AF842161

Renewing Your Mind as You Study Law

First Edition

Oak Brook College of Law and Government Policy
P.O. Box 26870, Fresno, CA 93729
www.obcl.edu

Printed in the United States of America
130130 5/13 Fourth Printing

ISBN 0-9713492-0-7

The Mission of Oak Brook College of Law and Government Policy

is to provide education and training in law and government policy in the context of a Biblical and historical framework; to prepare its students to take and pass the California Bar Examination and to prepare them professionally for the future practice of law; and to build and establish the Biblical foundations of truth, righteousness, justice, mercy, equity, integrity, and the fear of God in legal education and in the professional arenas of law and government policy.

Oak Brook College has adopted an approach to legal education that is different

both in form and in substance from that of other law schools. This new approach is not motivated simply by a desire to create something new for the sake of change, but rather was created in response to current concerns about the integrity of the legal profession and because of new technology that is revolutionizing educational methodology. Christian legal education, through its educational substance and methodology, emphasizes and reinforces Biblical standards of moral character.

A Biblical Worldview

Unless those in education look to the God of the Bible for standards of right and wrong, they cannot understand objective truth. Without objective truth, there can be no objective morality. That is why humanistic teaching results in moral relativism, where every man does that which is right in his own eyes. Legal education cannot be based upon moral relativism, because law, to be law, must be based upon certain, unchanging principles. Christian legal education approaches all moral and legal questions from the foundational premise that God is Creator, and thus we have a duty to enact laws and structure our legal systems in a manner consistent with His will. Our founders called the parameters for law and government "the Laws of Nature and of Nature's God."

"Training Advocates of Truth, Counselors of Reconciliation, and Ministers of Justice"

Table of Contents

WARNING

You are about to embark on an honorable, but dangerous, mission. It is honorable because the study of law prepares you to serve as a legal counselor and as an advocate for others. It is dangerous because there are many mental land mines and traps along the path of studying law. The risks are great! You could be deceived by worldly wisdom, and you could be subtly influenced to neglect or even to abandon your faith.

Many law students have compromised their faith as they consciously or unconsciously adopted wrong philosophies that are inherent within certain legal doctrines and practices. You must be alert and sober-minded during your study of the law, lest your heart be hardened through the deceitfulness of sin and your faith be shipwrecked.

You will need to pray for wisdom and discernment to recognize any error in legal and policy arguments. You will need to humble yourself before God so that you do not develop a proud and cynical attitude that can come with increased knowledge and legal training. Remember that God opposes the proud, but gives grace to the humble. His grace is sufficient as you acknowledge your weakness and ask Him to be glorified through your study.

The purpose of this book is to help you appreciate the need to have a right mind-set toward the study of law, a perspective and approach based upon Biblical principles. Three Scriptural dynamics are discussed: exposing the strongholds, renewing your mind, and putting on the character of Christ in your thoughts, words and actions. As you read the explanations and illustrations, you will comprehend the serious spiritual warfare and the current battlegrounds that exist in the legal profession.

The strongholds in law are just different manifestations of ungodly philosophies that have their origin in Satan, the father of all lies. Renewing one's mind is seeing things from God's perspective and allowing the Word to transform one's thinking. Being Christlike is our ultimate purpose in life. It involves taking on the character of Christ as the Holy Spirit enables us to respond properly to trials and tribulations. As we deny ourselves, the light of Christ is able to shine through us, and He enables us to do His work.

At Oak Brook College, we want each graduate to be more than a skilled professional. We want graduates who have the blessing of

God upon their lives because they walk in the Spirit and have appropriated God's promise of success to those who meditate on His Law day and night. We want lawyers who think and practice from a principled perspective, not from a pragmatic one. We want attorneys who can recognize and who will reject subtle, humanistic arguments that deny God's existence and sovereignty. We want advocates who are able to help others understand why Biblical/jurisdictional solutions to legal issues are far better than the current "balancing the interests" approach used by most courts. Finally, we want Oak Brook College graduates to be ***advocates of truth, counselors of reconciliation, and ministers of justice****.*

There is a desperate need for men and women in the legal profession who are willing to be "fools" for Christ and instruments of righteousness with wisdom that is pure and peaceable. We are grateful to God that He has called you to this challenge and level of service. We will pray that He Who is able to keep you from falling will guard your hearts and minds through Christ Jesus.

Robert J. Barth
Director of Academic Programs

Chapter One

Exposing the Strongholds

For though we walk in the flesh, we do not war after the flesh: (For the weapons of our warfare are not carnal, but mighty through God to the pulling down of strong holds;) Casting down imaginations, and every high thing that exalteth itself against the knowledge of God, and bringing into captivity every thought to the obedience of Christ. *II Corinthians 10:3–5*

Why is it so important to expose and pull down the strongholds in our study of law? It is essential because strongholds are lies. They are false perceptions. They have the appearance of truth and logic, but they lead to destruction. The study of law is ostensibly built on reason and logic, but our reason is corrupted and the passions of man are not pure. No matter how logical we try to be, our perceptions of truth can be distorted by our sins and the influence of others. Our "reason" can easily become a form of "rationalization" to justify our own desires and actions.

Reason is what led to the "Fall" of man in the Garden of Eden. Eve "saw" that the tree was good for food, and she was persuaded to forsake the truth because her reason and passion for "something better" seemed more "logical" than God's specific command.[1] God had told Adam and Eve that they would die if they ate the fruit of the tree of the knowledge of good and evil, but they had no understanding of the severity of the consequences. So it is with us in our personal lives and in the realm of legal doctrine. If something seems logical and beneficial, we can be deceived into doing things inconsistent with God's principles of justice and the truth. We can rationalize almost anything if we do not have hearts committed to the God of truth.

How many marriages have been destroyed because one or both partners have done what seemed or felt right? The rationalization that "I no longer love you" has been used by many to abandon their

[1]Genesis 3:1–6—"Now the serpent was more subtil than any beast of the field which the LORD God had made. And he said unto the woman, Yea, hath God said, Ye shall not eat of every tree of the garden? And the woman said unto the serpent, We may eat of the fruit of the trees of the garden: But of the fruit of the tree which is in the midst of the garden, God hath said, Ye shall not eat of it, neither shall ye touch it, lest ye die. And the serpent said unto the woman, Ye shall not surely die: For God doth know that in the day ye eat thereof, then your eyes shall be opened, and ye shall be as gods, knowing good and evil. And when the woman **saw** that the tree was good for food, and that it **was pleasant** to the eyes, and a tree **to be desired to make one wise**, she took of the fruit thereof, and did eat, and gave also unto her husband with her; and he did eat." (Emphasis added.)

vows of marriage, "till death do us part." Yet it is that very marital vow before God that is to keep a couple together during hard times. Trials are opportunities to strengthen and deepen a relationship, not a time to "bail out." The current deceptive attitude that if things do not work out we can just get a divorce is a self-fulfilling prophesy. If divorce is an "option" in a person's mind, it is only a matter of time before that option becomes a reality.

The law of sowing and reaping[2] is true, and it does not necessarily depend upon one's intentions. In fact, if one sows evil with good intentions, the fruit will still be evil. In the legal profession, certain philosophies and doctrines have been sown, and probably with good intentions, but because they were not examined in the light of God's truth, the long-term fruit has been very destructive. Now we find ourselves in the position of trying to undo the damage that has been done. These philosophies and doctrines are the "strongholds" that need to be exposed and torn down.

The wisest man who ever lived and the Master Teacher Himself, Jesus Christ, have made this truth clear. Solomon said, "There is a way that seemeth right unto a man, but the end thereof are the ways of death" (Proverbs 16:25). Jesus said, "I am the good shepherd," and "My sheep hear my voice" (John 10:11, 27). He also said, "He that entereth not by the door into the sheepfold, but climbeth up some other way, the same is a thief and a robber" (John 10:1), and "The thief cometh not, but for to steal, and to kill, and to destroy" (John 10:10). Jesus is "the way, the truth, and the life" (John 14:6), and He came so that we "might have life, and that [we] might have it more abundantly" (John 10:10).

If we, or any one else, makes decisions based upon perceptions, assumptions, and presuppositions that are not completely true, the result will be—at best—deception with a fragrance of truth. At worst, the fruit will be blatant evil justified as good. Based upon John 10:10, we can know that if we act or live by a lie in our personal lives, the fruit will be thievery, death, and destruction. It would be very naive to think that the same "cause-and-effect" dynamic is not also true when it comes to the study of law.

Using the old computer technology phrase "garbage in, garbage out" as an analogy, we need to be vigilant in our study of the law so that we do not allow "garbage" into our thinking that will poison our future thinking and actions. The foundations you lay in

---

[2]Galatians 6:7–8—"Be not deceived; God is not mocked: for whatsoever a man soweth, that shall he also reap. For he that soweth to his flesh shall of the flesh reap corruption; but he that soweth to the Spirit shall of the Spirit reap life everlasting."

your first year of legal study will be extremely difficult to destroy should you later realize that they are built on the shaky ground of humanistic philosophy or the quicksand of pragmatism.

If you are sober-minded and discerning, you are prepared to begin the treacherous journey of legal logic and reasoning. "The fear of the LORD is the beginning of wisdom: and the knowledge of the holy is understanding" (Proverbs 9:10). As you cling to that which is good and reject that which is evil,[3] you will maintain the right attitude for the study of law. As you commit your study to God and pray for wisdom, He will show you the subtle but destructive strongholds engrained in contemporary legal doctrines and their current, unjust fruit.[4]

The goal of this chapter is not to expose all the strongholds in legal thinking. It is only to highlight some of the false philosophies at the root of irrational court opinions, misleading study methods, and false legal philosophies. It is also to demonstrate why certain strongholds have had such devastating consequences in our current legal and political culture.

The Essence of a Stronghold

The Greek word for *stronghold* literally means "a castle," or figuratively it means "an argument, idea, presupposition." In legal study, a stronghold is a position or argument contrary to the will of God, or what William Blackstone called the "law of nature."[5] If we believe, or are even influenced by, a stronghold, we establish in our minds a pattern of thinking that eventually develops into a mental "castle" or paradigm through which we view current and future issues and events. Once established, a castle is not easily destroyed. It is fortified by habit, experience, and the affirmation of others. In the legal realm, court precedent, legislative action, and curriculum used in law schools can establish strongholds based upon false philosophies. Once a legal doctrine is established, it is very difficult to reverse, either legislatively or judicially.

Notice that II Corinthians 10:3–5 presumes that in our flesh we labor under strongholds. Yet God tells us that the weapons He has given us are not fleshly and thereby subject to the claims of the flesh, but that they are mighty through Him for the purpose of demolishing these strongholds. We must take every thought captive,

---

[3]Romans 12:9—"Let love be without dissimulation. Abhor that which is evil; cleave to that which is good."

[4]Proverbs 16:3—"Commit thy works unto the LORD, and thy thoughts shall be established."

[5]I WILLIAM BLACKSTONE, COMMENTARIES *39.

including ideas and philosophies, and examine them to see if they are consistent with the truth. This exercise is essential if we are going to think Biblically in the study of law.

How does one recognize these strongholds? As a Christian law student, your prayer should be that God would reveal to you any error in the legal material you are studying. You should pray as Solomon did for an understanding heart to discern between good and evil.[6] You will want to understand why the enemy's premises and strategies are wrong so that you can make judgments based upon truth and not be lulled into using wrong principles in an effort to accomplish "righteous" ends. Even if the use of pragmatic/humanistic reasoning produces short-term gains, the eventual outcome will be loss, because "God is not mocked." What may appear to be an immediate victory will later prove to be a long-term defeat.

God wants to reveal to you strongholds in your legal study as you cry out to Him for understanding. He promises that He will hear our cry and answer us.[7] We can be confident that the Holy Spirit is willing and able to convict the world of sin and lead us in all truth. With these promises as our foundation, let us examine some of the strongholds in the study of law.

Man Is the Only Source of Law

Years ago, leaders in our culture emphasized the importance of "obeying the law." Whether it was from parents, teachers, public officials or pastors, those in authority communicated societal standards and the moral reasons why the rules were so important. Generally, people appreciated the importance of the "golden rule" and understood that laws were for our general good. This was truth because the law was consistent with Biblical standards of morality.

Today, however, many people lack the moral foundation to understand the beneficial reasons for the rules, and they view commands, or the law, as an interference with their individual "liberty." Because of the educational focus on self-fulfillment, individual expression, and situational ethics, we have a generation with little respect for limitations on personal behavior, even when lawful restraint is necessary for societal order.

---

[6]I Kings 3:9—"Give therefore thy servant an understanding heart to judge thy people, that I may discern between good and bad: for who is able to judge this thy so great a people?"

[7]Psalm 50:15—"And call upon me in the day of trouble: I will deliver thee, and thou shalt glorify me." Psalm 86:7—"In the day of trouble I will call upon thee: for thou will answer me."

Absent a source of morality other than himself, man can view law as only rules dictated by those in power for reasons that are not necessarily known. The reasons could be honorable, but they also could be to please special interest groups, for personal gain, or to fulfill some personal agenda. This "power" view of law in a democratic system results in an acceptance that the majority is always "right," and it can lead to the oppression of individual freedoms.

On the other extreme, if individuality is elevated to the point where everyone becomes a law unto themselves, a type of anarchy results. Everyone does what is right in his own eyes, and there may be little respect for others or for future generations. This autonomous view feeds the attitude that "as long as I don't get caught, I'm O.K." One's moral restraint becomes limited to external forces, rather than internal control. This view will certainly lead to the downfall of a society, because the power of government can never control a people. As James Madison said, "We have staked the future of our political institutions upon the capacity of man-kind for self-government; upon the capacity of each and all of us to government [*sic*] ourselves . . . ."[8]

Both the "power" view of law and the libertarian-type view assume that man is the only source of law and is not subject to objective moral laws. The source is either those who have the "power" to make the rules, or the source is oneself. Each view (or variations thereof) ignores the self-evident truth held by our Founding Fathers that all men are **created** equal and that they are endowed by their Creator with certain unalienable rights. The fact that man is a created being necessarily implies that he is subject to the laws of the Creator, the "Laws of Nature and of Nature's God."[9]

After years of man-centered thinking and its incorporation into the law through legislation and judicial determinations, the result has often been unrighteous legal conclusions that cause us to ask, Where did we go wrong? or How did we get this far off? A few examples will help illustrate the way the stronghold consisting of the belief that man is the only source of law eventually reaps destructive results.

The now much-criticized Supreme Court decision, *Roe v. Wade*, still stands as binding authority for every court in the country. While a Supreme Court decision is not law, it has a similar effect because of the doctrine of *stare decisis* (adhering to decided cases). In that decision, the Court was confronted with the dilemma of "balancing"

---

[8]*America's God and Country Encyclopedia of Quotations* (W. Federer ed. 1994) 411.
[9]The Declaration of Independence para. 2 (U.S. 1776).

the interests of the state in protecting the unborn baby with the mother's "privacy rights."

In 1973, the Court gave more weight to the mother's "privacy rights" than it did to the duty of the state to protect life, or even the baby's right to life. If more weight had been given to life than to privacy, the "balance" would have come out differently. But the real problem was not the weight given to the various interests; the real problem was that the analysis was based upon a "balancing" of those interests. This approach is always dependent upon what interests the judges believe to be most important. The legal conclusion is subject to change as the importance of the relevant interests changes in the culture.

The view that law is reflective of culture was what a former dean of the Harvard Law School, Roscoe Pound, and others, called "sociological jurisprudence." The premise is that law must conform to the culture rather than the culture conform to the law. The former is an evolutionary/humanistic paradigm, while the latter is a historical and Biblical perspective. If one accepts the stronghold that man is the only source of law, he necessarily precludes the acknowledgment that there are objective moral laws apart from man.

Notice that the language of the *Roe v. Wade* decision expressly precluded the view that man's law must be interpreted consistently with an objective moral standard from a source other than man. In the United States, that objective standard is the "Laws of Nature and of Nature's God." Yet, Justice Blackmun, writing for the majority said:

> One's philosophy, one's experiences, one's exposure to the raw edges of human existence, one's religious training, one's attitudes toward life and family and their values, and the moral standards one establishes and seeks to observe, are all likely to influence and to color one's thinking and conclusions about abortion.
>
> In addition, population growth, pollution, poverty, and racial overtones tend to complicate and not to simplify the problem.
>
> Our task, of course, is to resolve the issue by constitutional measurement, free of emotion and of predilection.

Right after stating that the Court needed to look at the issue "free of emotion and of predilection," Justice Blackmun claimed that it would do this by looking to other men for counsel. He stated:

> We seek earnestly to do this, and, because we do, we have inquired into, and in this opinion place some emphasis upon, medical and medical-legal history and what that history reveals about man's attitudes toward the abortion procedure over the centuries.

The Court also considered the opinion of the American Medical Association, the American Public Health Association, and even the American Bar Association before reaching its conclusion that the right of privacy, whatever the source, "is broad enough to encompass a woman's decision whether or not to terminate her pregnancy."

With respect to the issue of whether the unborn baby was a person, the Court said it could decide the case without resolving "the difficult question of when life begins" because "the unborn have never been recognized in the law as persons in the whole sense."

The Court would have done well to listen to David's counsel in the Book of Psalms and to not listen to the counsel of the ungodly.[10] The Court attempted to base its decision upon the views of the "experts," but when experts cannot agree, as was the case in *Roe*, there is a real problem. Where, then, does the Court turn for answers? The judges are left to their own reason, influenced by their own predilections, emotions, and ignorance.

Consciously or unconsciously adhering to the view that man is the only source of law digs a deep rut in one's thinking that is extremely difficult to leave. To do so would require an admission that one's thinking previously had been wrong and would result in professional humiliation. The stronghold that man is the only source of law motivates one to justify himself and his views, even when they result in tragic consequences, as in *Roe v. Wade*, where the life of a human being is sacrificed on the altar of a mother's convenience, shame, or pride. Abortion is the ultimate example of a woman elevating her fears, desires, or will to the level of "law" such that it results in the termination of the yet-to-be-known person of unknown potential and creativity.

The dynamic of man elevating his "law" as supreme is not limited to the legal profession. It is true even in religious groups.

---

[10]Psalm 1:1—"Blessed is the man that walketh not in the counsel of the ungodly, nor standeth in the way of sinners, nor sitteth in the seat of the scornful."

Look what Jesus said about the Jewish leaders who elevated the traditions of men over the Law of God.

> Why do ye also transgress the commandment of God by your tradition? For God commanded, saying, Honour thy father and mother: and, He that curseth father or mother, let him die the death. But ye say, Whosoever shall say to his father or his mother, It is a gift, by whatsoever thou mightest be profited by me; And honour not his father or his mother, he shall be free. Thus have ye made the commandment of God of none effect by your tradition. Ye hypocrites, well did Esaias prophesy of you, saying, This people draweth nigh unto me with their mouth, and honoureth me with their lips; but their heart is far from me. But in vain they do worship me, teaching for doctrines the commandments of men (Matthew 15:3–9).

Just as lawyers in the legal profession end up justifying themselves when they are deceived into thinking that man is the only source of law, lawyers or experts in the Jewish law also justified themselves so that they could excuse themselves from obeying God's Law.[11]

Consider the parable of the Good Samaritan. It was an expert in the law who wanted to justify himself by asking Jesus, "Who is my neighbor?" Jesus responded with the parable to force the expert to realize that a "neighbor" included even the socially outcast people of the day and that our duty is to show mercy (love) toward all people.[12]

A modern manifestation of the stronghold that man is the only source of law is the movement to expand the definition of marriage to include sodomite relationships. In the Hawaii Supreme Court case that popularized this issue, the court essentially said that the state has the power to redefine this God-ordained relationship.

> The power to regulate marriage is a sovereign function reserved exclusively to the respective states. By its very nature, the power to regulate the marriage relation includes the power to determine the requisites of a valid marriage contract and to control the qualifications of

[11]Luke 11:46—"Woe unto you also, ye lawyers! for ye lade men with burdens grievous to be borne, and ye yourselves touch not the burdens with one of your fingers."

[12]Luke 10:36–37—"Which now of these three, thinkest thou, was neighbor unto him that fell among the thieves? And he said, He that shewed mercy on him. Then said Jesus unto him, Go, and do thou likewise."

> the contracting parties, the forms and procedures necessary to solemnize the marriage, the duties and obligations it creates, its effect upon property and other rights, and the grounds for marital dissolution.

Baehr v. Lewin, 852 P.2d 44, 46–47 (Haw. 1993).

The court then elevated the concept of equality to the point that it trumped the truth that there are legitimate distinctions between males and females when it comes to marriage eligibility. Based upon the view that marriage is a "state-conferred legal status," the court stated:

> [Hawaii Revised Statute] § 572-1, on its face, discriminates based on sex against the applicant couples in the exercise of the **civil right of marriage**, thereby implicating the equal protection clause of article I, section 5 of the Hawaii Constitution.
>
> The equal protection clauses of the United States and Hawaii Constitutions are not mirror images of one another . . . . Hawaii's counterpart is more elaborate. Article I, section 5 of the Hawaii Constitution provides in relevant part that "[n]o person shall be denied the equal protection of the laws, nor be denied the enjoyment of the person's civil rights or be discriminated against in the exercise thereof because of race, religion, sex or ancestry." Thus, by its plain language, the Hawaii Constitution prohibits state-sanctioned discrimination against any person in the exercise of his or her **civil rights** on the basis of sex.

Baehr v. Lewin, 852 P.2d at 51, 53 (Haw. 1993) (emphasis added).

The path of reprobation does not stop with wrongly decided court decisions, but has escalated to a point where another state supreme court essentially ordered the state legislature to create a "separate but equal" form of marriage for sodomite couples. These "civil unions," as they are now called under Vermont law, are only the next step in a strategy to have sodomite relationships receive the same legitimacy as traditional marriages.

It is instructive to look at the language of the Vermont Supreme Court opinion to see how the court clearly framed its analysis within the perspective that man is the only source of law.

> May the State of Vermont exclude same-sex couples from the benefits and protections that its laws provide to opposite-sex married couples? That is the fundamental question we address in this appeal, a question that the court well knows arouses deeply felt religious, moral, and political beliefs. Our constitutional responsibility to consider the legal merits of issues properly before us provides no exception for the controversial case. The issue before the court, moreover, does not turn on the religious or moral debate over intimate same-sex relationships, but rather on the statutory and constitutional basis for the exclusion of same-sex couples from the secular benefits and protections offered married couples.

Baker v. State of Vermont, 744 A.2d 864, 867 (Vt. 1999).

After going through its "reasoned" analysis, the Vermont Court concluded:

> Thus, viewed in the light of history, logic, and experience, we conclude that none of the interests asserted by the State provides a reasonable and just basis for the continued exclusion of same-sex couples from the benefits incident to a civil marriage license under Vermont law.

Baker v. State of Vermont, 744 A.2d at 886 (Vt. 1999).

Emasculated by the erroneous view that because the state supreme court said it, it is law and must be accepted without question, the Vermont legislature worked swiftly so as not to experience the reproof of the court for not obeying its "command." Guided by their own reason and the political pressures of gay and lesbian supporters, the majority of the legislators saw nothing wrong with legalizing sodomite relationships and creating a legal framework that puts this abomination on an "equal" basis as a marriage between a male and a female. Thus, we now have "civil unions" along with marriages in the state of Vermont, but it will not stop there. Similar efforts are under way in Massachusetts and other states to "legitimize" sodomite relationships.

We can see from these few examples how the seemingly innocuous idea that man is the only source of law eventually has profound consequences in our legal and political framework. Such a perspective is rooted in humanism and evolutionary philosophy. Within the judicial, legislative, and executive authorities, we can see numerous examples of how so-called legal scholars have been seduced, as Eve was, into believing that man can decide for himself what is the best way. Despite the law written on their hearts, lawyers often advocate positions that violate what they would do "personally," because the position is either the "law" as man has determined, or it is how they want the law to be, to best serve their client's selfish interests. The stronghold that man is the only source of law is a poison that may be tasteless or even sweet at first, but the long-term implications are perverse and deadly.

Fairness Is the Same as Justice

With the study of law, as with all communication, semantics are important. What one intends to communicate may not be what another perceives by the words used. *Fairness* is one of those semantically sticky words. *Fairness* can have either a subjective or an objective connotation, depending on one's understanding of the nature of law versus equity.

Black's Law Dictionary defines *fair* as "equitable as a basis for exchange; reasonable; a fair value; impartial, free from suspicion, bias, etc.; just; equitable; even-handed; equal as between conflicting interests." Thus, when we are dealing with a commercial exchange, *fairness* means reasonable value. When one is speaking about a decision maker, *fair* means without partiality and unbiased toward the parties involved or the issues. If there is a conflict between competing interests, *fairness* connotes a compromise where both parties receive some of what they were seeking.

Now, contrast the concept of fairness with the concept of justice. *Black's Law Dictionary* defines *just* as "conforming to or consonant with, what is legal or lawful, legally right, lawful. Correct, true, due. Right; in accordance with law and justice."

Many people consider fairness to be the same as justice, but there is a profound difference. From the dictionary definitions alone, one can see that fairness becomes relevant when there is no real legal standard and an equitable decision must be made to resolve the issue. But justice always involves the application of a specific legal standard to a factual situation to determine what is right in that situation. Today, however, concepts of fairness are being used where principles of justice are needed. In many cases, the evasive "fairness" doctrine has swallowed up principles of justice to the point that legal decisions are only a matter of "balancing the interests" of the parties. From this perspective, judges often interpose their "sense of fairness" into their decisions when the facts and law require the imposition of justice.

If a defendant is clearly guilty of murder, people would be outraged if a judge ruled that the defendant was not guilty just because the defendant had a "hard life." The guilt or innocence of a crime is not a decision of equity that involves balancing the interests of the victim and the perpetrator. There are clear standards that must be followed to decide if the defendant committed, beyond a reasonable doubt, the criminal act.

While it is true that judges have some discretion in sentencing someone convicted of a crime, that discretion is not an exercise in "balancing the interests" to determine guilt. Rather, it is a judgment of what is the appropriate sanction based upon the seriousness of the wrong committed and the blameworthiness of the defendant. One who intentionally injures someone and shows no signs of repentance or remorse should receive a more severe sanction than one who accidentally causes the same type of injury.

While understanding the difference between fairness and justice seems easy in the context of a criminal action involving the physical injury of another, the concepts have been confused and perverted in other areas involving legal, rather than equitable, issues. In fact, what are in essence "equitable considerations" are sometimes wrongly used in cases when legal principles should control. An example of where this can happen is in the areas of family and juvenile law.

Best Interests of the Child Test

The most frequent application of the equitable "best interests of the child" test is in divorce/custody cases where the parents cannot agree on the custody of the children. In such situations, the judge has the responsibility to determine what placement would be in the best interests of each child. It is extremely important that the judge make his decision consistent with the objective standard of the laws of nature and of nature's God. Otherwise, the judge will act as if he is the source of law and will make his decision based upon his own standard of morality and his own predilections.

Absent an objective standard of morality, we see judges placing a child in the custody of a parent who has an immoral lifestyle rather than one who is religious and who would try to raise the child according to Biblical standards of right and wrong. We see judges deciding that it is not in the best interests of the child to be "sheltered" or "indoctrinated" by the religious parent. The child is placed in the care of the parent with whom the child will have more opportunities to experience life and become "well-rounded."

Therefore, even when an equitable approach such as the best interests of the child test is appropriate, a judge may not act as if he is the source of law. Even decisions in equity must be based upon fixed principles of morality if the result is going to be truly "fair."

The best interests of the child standard is also used in juvenile cases when the court must decide the placement of children. These cases often involve allegations of neglect or abuse. It is in these cases that the equitable best interests of the child test is often misapplied because legal principles should control.

Abuse and neglect are serious matters because they involve the unalienable rights of a child. According to the Declaration of Independence, the purpose of government is to protect and secure the people's unalienable rights. Children as well as adults have unalienable rights. If a parent does something to infringe upon the unalienable right to life of the child, the civil government's jurisdiction is triggered, and the parent must be treated as any other person accused of a crime. If a parent, or any one else, endangers a child's life or physical well-being (properly defined abuse and neglect) the parent/child relationship may be affected because of the state's duty to protect life. However, absent such a violation of a child's unalienable rights, the parent/child relationship should remain intact, regardless of what a judge may think is in the best interests of the child. Government must respect the family jurisdiction, and social workers should not be allowed to usurp the legal principle of parental authority by using the best interests of the child as a threat.

A statute common in many state Juvenile Codes illustrates the tragic results that can occur when parental authority is supplanted by what the state thinks is best for the child. Under existing statutory schemes, a child can refuse to live at home, and the state prosecutor is authorized to file a Petition for Authoritative Intervention. The child can be placed in foster care under the custody of the Department of Social Services until there is a hearing on temporary custody. This happens even when there are not allegations of abuse or neglect. Eventually the court determines the placement of the child based upon the best interests of the child test.

What is so damaging to the authority of the family in such situations is that the child essentially calls the shots. If the child refuses to live at home because the parents are "too restrictive" or will not let the child participate in certain social activities, the court must make a decision on what is in the best interests of the child. This is true even if there is no abuse or neglect involved, but only the child's desires and rebellious nature.

Such situations put the parents in the position of trying to justify their authority, as if the child was owned by the state. Parenting becomes a privilege granted by the state rather than a God-ordained responsibility. The correct legal view is that unless there is physical abuse or neglect involved, the state has no authority to use the best interests test to decide the placement of a child. The child belongs at home under the authority of his parents who are accountable to God for how they train their children.

Compelling State Interest Test

When the stronghold that "fairness" is the same as "justice" is accepted, the use of balancing of interests tests becomes more prevalent. This is true even in the area of constitutional law. Since the 1960s, the compelling state interest test has been used when a statute is challenged as violating someone's equal protection and due process rights, or one's "fundamental rights," such as the freedom of religion. Sometimes, however, the compelling state interest test is not used, and the Supreme Court uses an approach that looks at the nature and legitimacy of the interests involved.

An example of the balancing approach is *Wisconsin v. Yoder*, 406 U.S. 205 (1972). In this case, the Court's majority opinion insisted that "a state's interest in universal education" must be balanced "when it impinges on fundamental rights and interests." The facts involved an Amish gentleman who was convicted of violating Wisconsin's mandatory education law for not sending his fifteen-year-old daughter to school after she completed the eighth grade. The Amish culture objects to high school education because of their "fundamental belief that salvation requires life in church community separate and apart from the world and worldly influence."

The Court ruled that the conviction must be overturned because it violated the free exercise clause. The Court said, "Only those interests of the highest order and those not otherwise served can overbalance legitimate claims of free exercise." The state could not prevail unless it showed that its requirement did not "deny the free exercise of religious beliefs" and that there was "a state interest of sufficient magnitude to override the [free exercise claim]."

By the compelling state interest test, a court looks to see if the state or government has a compelling interest in the area regulated. The state must demonstrate that it has not only the constitutional authority and a compelling reason to make laws in the area, but also that there are no less restrictive means to accomplish the interest of the state. In other words, the state must first show that the regulated activity is within the jurisdiction of the government, and then, that the method or scope of regulation was the least restrictive to the plaintiff's constitutional rights. Only if the state can satisfy both of these elements will the challenged statute or practice be deemed constitutionally permissible.

It is easy to see the balancing of interests being done by using this test. The interests of the state are being balanced against the alleged constitutional rights of the individual plaintiff. In *Yoder*, the interests of the Amish prevailed.

Now let us look at a different example. Suppose a state passes a law making it illegal to possess, sell, or ingest the hallucinatory drug peyote. The state passes such a law on the basis that the legislation is necessary to protect lives, both those that may want to use peyote and those that could be affected by those who use it. Now, also suppose that a particular Indian tribe uses peyote in its religious rituals. The question that is raised is, Does the statute violate the Indians' religious freedom?

If the compelling state interest test was used to decide this issue, the court would look to see if the state had a compelling interest in regulating the use of drugs such as peyote. If the state was able to convince the court that it did, the state would then have to demonstrate that it could not accomplish its goals in a way that was less restrictive to the Indians' alleged religious rights.

A case involving these facts actually reached the United States Supreme Court in *Employment Division v. Smith*, 495 U.S. 872, 110 S.Ct. 1595 (1990). To the surprise of many legal scholars, the Court said that the compelling state interest test was inapplicable. The Court resolved this case by using jurisdictional principles, and it decided that the state had a legitimate interest in promulgating criminal laws against the use of drugs. As long as the law did not specifically target the religious practices of the Indians, the statute did not violate the Indians' right to free exercise of religion.

The Court said, "We have never held that an individual's religious beliefs excuse him from compliance with an otherwise valid law prohibiting conduct that the State is free to regulate." In fact, the Court stated, "To make an individual's obligation to obey such a law contingent upon the law's coincidence with his religious beliefs, except where the State's interest is 'compelling'—permitting him, by virtue of his beliefs, 'to become a law unto himself,'—contradicts both constitutional tradition and common sense."

In *Smith*, the Court relied on previous cases that dealt with the religious practice of bigamy as authority for its decision regarding the religious practice of ingesting peyote. In the bigamy cases, the Supreme Court had upheld state statutes that outlawed bigamy, even when it was practiced as part of the Mormon religion.

The real point to this section is not to discuss issues within family law or constitutional law, but it is to point out that fairness and justice are different concepts in the law. Both are involved in resolving issues, but they require different approaches and presuppositions. With a balancing of interests approach there is greater subjectivity at each level of inquiry. For example, by what standard does the court decide that the state's interest is compelling? In the Vermont case dealing with sodomite marriages, the state supreme court decided that the state's interest in protecting the legitimacy of the traditional marriage relationship was not compelling. In *Roe v. Wade*, the United States Supreme Court decided that Texas's interest in protecting life, albeit unborn, was not compelling.

Balancing of interest tests often result in decisions based upon evolving standards, and legal questions being converted into equitable ones to reach a "fair" result based upon the times. Every law student and lawyer should be alert to the potential deception of the balancing of interests tests that often equate fairness with justice.

Strongholds Within Litigation

The word *litigation* comes from words meaning a contest or debate. It literally means to contest at law, to prosecute or defend by pleadings, or an exhibition of evidence and judicial debate. The concept certainly connotes conflict, differences of opinion, and opposing positions not reconciled by other means.

Litigation communicates an image of a battle, a dispute in which the attorneys are the "hired guns" that act as mouthpieces for the opposing parties. This picture communicates that there is a winner and a loser. One party is victorious and the other defeated. Is this an arena in which a Christian can participate? Did not Jesus say to "love your enemies"?[13]

For Christians who enjoy debate, conflict, and litigation, one has to question their motives, for Proverbs tells us that "only by pride cometh contention." Yet, for Christians who make efforts to avoid all conflicts or discussion of issues, one has to question their commitment to the truth, because the second half of the same verse says, "but with the well advised is wisdom" (Proverbs 13:10).

[13]Matthew 5:44—"But I say unto you, Love your enemies, bless them that curse you, do good to them that hate you, and pray for them which despitefully use you, and persecute you."

Proverbs also says, “They that forsake the law praise the wicked, but such as keep the law contend with them” (Proverbs 28:4). This verse says that sometimes it is necessary to go into a legal battle in order to ferret out truth. Scripture gives us many examples of people not telling the truth because of fear, pride, selfish ambition, or some other reason.

Cross-examination in litigation is a Biblical way to bring out the truth. “He that is first in his own cause seemeth just; but his neighbour cometh and searcheth him” (Proverbs 18:17).

The truth that pulls down strongholds within litigation is “wisdom.” The proclamation of wisdom and truth is the Biblical and correct perspective on conflict and litigation. A Christian attorney should not have a win/lose attitude or a contentious attitude, but he should be an advocate for the truth, presenting it in a way that is “peaceable” and “easy to be entreated.”

Consider these verses:

> Mercy and truth are met together; righteousness and peace have kissed each other. Truth shall spring out of the earth; and righteousness shall look down from heaven (Psalm 85:10–11).
>
> Who is a wise man and endued with knowledge among you? let him show out of a good conversation his works with meekness of wisdom (James 3:13).
>
> But if ye have bitter envying and strife in your hearts, glory not, and lie not against the truth. This wisdom descendeth not from above, but is earthly, sensual, and devilish. For where envying and strife is, there is confusion and every evil work (James 3:14–16).
>
> But the wisdom that is from above is first pure, then peaceable, gentle, and easy to be entreated, full of mercy and good fruits, without partiality, and without hypocrisy. And the fruit of righteousness is sown in peace of them that make peace (James 3:17–18).

One cannot read these verses once and receive their full meaning. One must read and reread them. Only by meditating on their meaning can one understand the power that comes from acting and speaking with wisdom from above. After one studies these passages, a few principles applicable to "litigation" are clear. These principles destroy the worldly, television image of litigation many of us knowingly or unknowingly have. These principles give the right perspective on conflicts for righteous causes. As Christian lawyers, we are not called to be "litigators," but we are called to be advocates of truth, counselors of reconciliation, and ministers of justice.

Let us consider some of the truths that can be drawn from those verses.

1. There is earthly, sensual wisdom, and there is Godly wisdom. These opposing types of wisdom can be clearly seen in different approaches or philosophies on a topic.

2. The two types of wisdom can be distinguished in litigation by certain characteristics. Earthly wisdom involves striving and envying and has a focus on winning. Godly wisdom is based upon truth. It is peaceable, easily understood, and easy to be entreated. The focus of Godly wisdom is justice, equality, and mercy; the focus is not on winning.

3. Conventional counsel regarding litigation techniques and strategies are worldly. These views need to be exposed and rejected in the light of Godly wisdom.

For some people, even the thought of civil litigation causes tension. This could be for several reasons, most of which are worldly. One possible reason is that the individual views a trial as a game of who has the best strategy to win, even if the strategy involves deception. Another reason could be that one sees court proceedings as confrontations between individuals. The courtroom is perceived as a place of great personal vulnerability in which the attorney is being observed, and even judged, rather than being the place where facts are determined and righteous causes argued.

How does one overcome the fear of man (loss of reputation) that often inhibits one from doing trial work? How does one pull down the false idea (stronghold) that a trial is a personal battle between the attorneys? This can be done only by surrendering one's reputation to God and dying to self. Also, one must be convinced that he is advocating a righteous cause or representing a person who has a righteous claim. If these two conditions are not there, the attorney should use other efforts to bring about reconciliation and a just result between parties who are in conflict.

There are certainly other personal and professional strongholds that can affect a person's view of and performance within litigation. But if one seeks the truth and acts in a spirit of meekness, the liberty and power to be an effective advocate will be present.

Law Is Only an Instrument to Accomplish a Desired Result

Early in one's study of law, a student must recognize that there is a difference between the "descriptive" and the "prescriptive." The Latin terms *de facto* and *de jure* are often used to articulate the difference between what is, *de facto*, and the way things should be, *de jure*. *De jure* means, "of right," "legitimate," or "lawful." A law student must learn to describe and articulate existing facts, and he must also learn to ask and answer prescriptive questions. How should things be? If they are not that way, why not, and what can be done about it?

The key question for a law student and an attorney is what makes a law *de jure*, legitimate or right? Is it legitimate only because there was a properly enacted law? Not necessarily. Even the "prescriptive" can be "wrong." A statute can be properly enacted by a state legislature and still be illegitimate, either on constitutional grounds, or on the grounds that it violates the laws of nature. This analysis of determining whether a law is legitimate really relates back to the discussion of the stronghold that man is the only source of law. If the end or purpose of the law is not legitimate, then the fact that it was properly enacted does not make it right. There must be an objective standard that controls whether the purpose of a law is legitimate. This concept of an objective legal standard is discussed more thoroughly in the next chapter.

If one separates the law from the legitimacy question, law becomes only an instrument or tool to be used by those in power to accomplish the goals they desire. If this pragmatic view is held, the legitimacy of the goals is not a question. The only issue is whether the law was properly enacted by the prescribed method. Law, then, is viewed only as a means to accomplish what are often self-serving and partisan interests.

A classic Biblical example of this pragmatic, instrumentalist view of law is the law of the Medes and the Persians. Remember when King Darius's officials conspired to destroy Daniel but could find no fault in him? These men flattered Darius and persuaded him to decree that no one was allowed to pray to anyone but Darius for thirty days. No consideration was made as to whether such a decree was right or wrong, or whether the king had the authority to make such a decree. It was pleasing to the king and thus it was decreed.

This mentality is typical in a democratic culture. Law becomes what the majority wants or what the "king" desires or is persuaded to do in an attempt to either please some interest group or to serve selfish desires. The point is that if law is only an instrument, anything could become law if enacted in the prescribed way.

We see this dynamic becoming more and more prevalent in our culture today. Partisan politics, political action committees, lobbying groups, and special interest groups try to persuade legislators to enact legislation consistent with their agenda. Because of the self-interest for reelection, many legislators succumb to the pressure and vote in a way justified as "representing the will of the people." Such a paradigm is not that of a representative republic in which we live. We need statesmen and judges who are willing to be courageous to uphold principles that are truly in the best interest of the people, and who will not capitulate to those who want to reduce the nature of law down to pragmatic and selfish politics.

Will the stronghold that law is only an instrument affect how you study law? Of course it will. Let me give you a few examples. In tort law today, the concept of individual fault has been eliminated in certain types of injuries. In worker compensation cases, as long as the employee was injured while performing his job, it does not matter if the employer was negligent. The statutes dictate the amount of compensation the employee may recover. This was a "law" properly enacted and heavily supported by industry to limit the liability of employers when employees are injured on the job, even when the employer is clearly negligent.

Another example of law being used only as an instrument is no-fault auto insurance. The issue of fault is irrelevant. The only issues are damages and how much the insured person will have to pay. As with many tort reform proposals, the key policy questions have been how can the anticipated losses be best spread over the industry, and who is the best person to pay for the losses? Here, the principle of individual responsibility is abandoned, and the law is enacted to "spread the costs" over a larger group of people.

We even see this instrumentalist approach in the area of constitutional law. Congress has passed many laws that are not for any of the purposes articulated in Article I, Section 8 of the Constitution. Federal tax dollars are being spent on the arts, social welfare, education, and even on fetal research because there are enough legislators who believe that these issues are "national concerns." The federal courts have justified them on the basis that they "affect commerce" or are related to the "general welfare" of the nation. The law has been used to accomplish what those in power wanted, even if the objects or goals of these laws are not within the purposes authorized by the Constitution.

So, as you study law, beware of the manifestations of the stronghold that law is only a tool to manipulate culture to a more "enlightened" state. Do not be lulled into thinking the only thing that matters is if the majority wants it, or that it will help to accomplish some "good." Always ask the question whether the law is being used lawfully.

The Stronghold of Comparison

As with every deception, the stronghold of comparison sounds reasonable and may even contain an element of truth. Yet, as many students have experienced, the stronghold of comparison has devastating consequences.

We are instructed in Scripture to be "like-minded"[14] and to "be followers,"[15] but we are also told that it is wrong to compare ourselves with others.[16] How can these verses be reconciled? Comparison is not wrong in itself. We err only when we compare the wrong things. We all understand why it is not appropriate to compare apples with oranges. Such a comparison has no credibility, because it involves two things that are not comparable. They are so dissimilar in nature that the analysis is a contrast rather than a comparison. Yet, how often do we give great credibility to comparisons that are as equally not comparable?

The examples are numerous. Parents compare their children; brothers and sisters compare themselves to each other; students compare themselves to other students; professionals compare themselves to other professionals; ministers compare themselves with other ministers—and the list goes on.

Not only do we, as unique individuals created in God's image, compare ourselves to others, but we also compare ourselves for wrong reasons. We compare ourselves with others to justify our actions

---

[14]Philippians 2:2—"Fulfill ye my joy, that ye be like-minded, having the same love, being of one accord, of one mind."

[15]I Corinthians 4:16—"Wherefore I beseech you, be ye followers of me." Philippians 3:17—"Brethren, be followers together of me, and mark them which walk so as ye have us for an ensample."

[16]II Corinthians 10:12—"For we dare not make ourselves of the number, or compare ourselves with some that commend themselves: but they measuring themselves by themselves, and comparing themselves among themselves, are not wise."

based on the fact that "others are doing it." We compare ourselves to others to make us feel better about our own faults and inadequacies. We even compare ourselves with others for selfish gain in position or wealth.

In the academic realm, comparisons can be very destructive to those who do not "make the grade" or who are not "gifted." The pressure to perform and the emotional defeat that occurs from not meeting the expectations are real and must be addressed if one is to be free from this stronghold. While "grades" may be a necessary evil in our culture, both the student's and the teacher's attitudes toward the evaluation of subject-matter comprehension must be based upon truth.

First of all, the only One with whom we should compare ourselves is Jesus Christ. We are to be "like-minded" with Him and take on the role of a servant. As His bond servant, we are to do all things for Him and for His glory.[17] This comparison will never lead to self-condemnation or condemnation from God, because He is love and love never condemns. In fact, this comparison and identification with Christ results in liberty and enthusiasm. The joy that comes from serving is a gift from God, designed to benefit us and others.

Satan wants us to make comparisons so that we will judge and criticize ourselves and others. Satan even uses our own Christianity to condemn us because we are not always Christlike. We need to affirm that Christianity is not based upon works, but it is based upon our faith in the finished work of Christ. The Apostle Paul tells us the only thing that matters is faith working or expressing itself through love.[18] This leads to good works, but our faith cannot be based upon good works. We are not saved by works, but rather we are saved to *do* good works so that the Father is glorified.[19] Satan wants us to believe that our status as Christians depends on our works, but God says that our relationship with Him is based on our faith and love. What a contrast, and yet we all, to some degree, are deceived by the stronghold of comparison. When we are deceived by this stronghold, we experience its fruits, which are theft, death, and destruction.[20]

---

[17]Colossians 3:17—"And whatsoever ye do in word and deed, do all in the name of the Lord Jesus, giving thanks to God and the Father by him." Colossians 3:23–24—"And whatsoever ye do, do it heartily, as to the Lord, and not unto men; Knowing that of the Lord ye shall receive the reward of the inheritance: for ye serve the Lord Christ."

[18]Galatians 5:6—"For in Jesus Christ neither circumcision availeth any thing nor uncircumcision; but faith which worketh by love."

[19]Matthew 5:16—"Let your light so shine before men, that they may see your good works, and glorify your Father which is in heaven."

[20]John 10:10a—"The thief cometh not, but for to steal, and to kill, and to destroy."

Jesus told us, "Judge not, and ye shall not be judged: condemn not, and ye shall not be condemned: forgive, and ye shall be forgiven" (Luke 6:37). In the negative, this means that if we judge (wrong comparisons), we will feel judged, whether or not anyone openly judges us. If we condemn, we will feel condemned—either by others or by self-condemnation. If we do not forgive, we will not feel forgiven.

As law students and as lawyers, we need to cry out to God, asking Him to open our eyes to the deception of the enemy in the area of comparisons. From a personal perspective, we must expose and resist the stronghold of comparison with respect to our relationships with others and to the things others have. Any improper elevation in our sight of people or things is idolatry, rooted in lust and envy. Be assured, where there is envy and strife, there is confusion and every evil work.[21] Comparison rooted in envy and strife is certainly not the mind-set that God desires for us. He wants us to eliminate all anxiety that comes from comparisons by humbling ourselves and admitting our need for His provision.[22] The result will be "the peace that passes all understanding,"[23] and the fruit will be the "pure and peaceable"[24] wisdom that is from above.

From an academic standpoint, one must guard against comparisons of grades, oratory ability, and trial skills. Law school is a training ground in which everyone receives the same training, but no one is called to exactly the same ministry of reconciliation and justice. The training will equip some to be better mothers or fathers; God will use others in the governmental arena; others will serve the general public in small office practices; some will be called to be public advocates. Regardless of where God places you, be assured that He will equip you to do the good works He ordained for you.[25]

---

[21]James 3:14–16—"But if ye have bitter envying and strife in your hearts, glory not, and lie not against the truth. This wisdom descendeth not from above, but is earthly, sensual, devilish. For where envying and strife is, there is confusion and every evil work."

[22]I Peter 5:6–7—"Humble yourselves therefore under the mighty hand of God, that he may exalt you in due time: Casting all your care upon him; for he careth for you." II Corinthians 12:9—"And he said unto me, My grace is sufficient for thee: for my strength is made perfect in weakness. Most gladly therefore will I rather glory in my infirmities, that the power of Christ may rest upon me.

[23]Philippians 4:6–7—"Be careful for nothing; but in everything by prayer and supplication with thanksgiving let your requests be made known unto God. And the peace of God, which passeth all understanding, shall keep your hearts and minds through Christ Jesus."

[24]James 3:17—"But the wisdom that is from above is first pure, then peaceable, gentle, and easy to be entreated, full of mercy and good fruits, without partiality, and without hypocrisy."

[25]Ephesians 2:10—"For we are his workmanship, created in Christ Jesus unto good works, which God hath before ordained that we should walk in them."

Be warned, however, that making wrong comparisons among your fellow students and others can greatly delay the "ordination" to do those good works, because before you can be a true servant in any area, God will have to first deal with your character and expose the stronghold of comparison in your life. Jesus came to seek and save that which was lost.[26] He shed His blood that we might experience redemption and freedom from the bondage of sin, including the stronghold of comparison.

A true servant looks up to God for strength and direction, and he looks around for opportunities to love and be a minister of truth. If you, as a student, tear down the stronghold of comparison now, you will be able to serve with liberty as a lawyer and help destroy the castles in the legal profession that have been built upon the stronghold of comparison. God may be calling you to expose the "towers of Babel" in the legal profession, some of which are rooted in comparisons based upon man's standards.

Equal Protection

Some of the case precedents and laws in the area of equal protection are good legal examples of false comparisons. When the Supreme Court of Vermont ruled that the statute limiting marriage licenses to male/female couples was unconstitutional, it was on the basis that the statute violated the "common benefits" clause of the Vermont Constitution. The court ruled that the state could not grant a marriage license to a heterosexual couple, while refusing to grant it to a homosexual couple. To do so, the court said, denied the homosexual couple equal benefits under the law of the state.

The denial of equal benefits is the flip side of the denial of equal protection. The denial of equal benefits results in some people receiving benefits not received by others, and denying equal protection deprives some people of legal protection given to others. The post-Civil War amendments to benefit and protect African-Americans involved both concepts. The "privileges and immunities" clause in the Fourteenth Amendment was designed to declare that African-Americans shall have the "equal benefits" or the unalienable rights enjoyed by every citizen in the United States, and the "equal protection" clause ensured that the African-Americans would receive the same legal protection as others when it came to their life, liberty, and property.

Following is the key question we should ask when it comes to legal comparisons: What is being compared? Are we comparing

---

[26]Luke 19:10—"For the Son of man is come to seek and to save that which was lost."

apples and oranges, or two of the same fruit? With respect to slavery, the stronghold was that African-Americans were not human, or if they were, they were not in the same class as other humans. Thus, many justified treating African-Americans differently because it was not inappropriate to make distinctions between two different types of beings. It was an apple/orange distinction, if you will. Obviously, that comparison was wrong and needed to be corrected legally. The law needed to be changed to give African-Americans equal opportunity and equal protection under the law.

The "equal protection" clause has been used in a wide variety of cases in which someone is claiming "unequal treatment" rather than unequal protection. The concepts of equal protection and the due process clauses have evolved into a view that these clauses require equality of results or position rather than the original intent of equality of opportunity. If there is a disparity, many advocate that the government should use the "law" to correct the socioeconomic "inequality." One can easily see that this form of comparison and legal response is the foundation for socialism and its goal of redistributing the wealth so that everyone is more "equal."

With respect to the Vermont case, the court never seriously considered that there might be a legitimate reason to make a distinction between homosexual couples and heterosexual couples. While lawyers for the state made an attempt to "justify the distinction," the court ignored their arguments concerning family and child rearing because the state had already passed a law allowing homosexual couples to adopt children. The lawyers never argued that the distinction is proper and necessary because of the laws of nature regarding sexual relationships.

This case not only illustrates the dangers of the stronghold of comparison, but it also further illuminates the pervasiveness of the stronghold that man is the only source of law. No one even raised the position that marriage is a God-ordained institution and that to violate the laws of nature results in the judgment of God.[27]

Another example of the stronghold of comparison is in the area of employment. Most would probably agree that equal pay for equal work is a good principle for employers to follow, but what about equal pay for "comparable work"? There have been legal scholars and legislators who have argued that a state should develop

---

[27]Leviticus 18: 22, 24–25—"Thou shalt not lie with mankind, as with womankind: it is abomination. . . . Defile not ye yourselves in any of these things: for in all these the nations are defiled which I cast out before you: And the land is defiled: therefore I do visit the iniquity thereof upon it, and the land itself vomiteth out her inhabitants."

a master schedule and classify all types of work into several categories. The purpose of such an effort would be to determine what jobs would be "comparable" and should receive the same or similar compensation. The theory is that a nurse, for example, may contribute comparably to an accountant and therefore should be paid the same. Those in authority would make the determination of comparable values of jobs, and the compensation level would be mandated based upon the master schedule. This legal effort in "employment equality" certainly has not been imposed upon private employers, but a form of this "comparable worth" concept is the practice among some public employers around the country.

Much could be said about the legal implications of comparisons between men and women. From employment opportunities, military service, education opportunities, and harassment charges, the environment for wrong comparisons is ripe. As with other areas of comparison, the important question is, On what basis is the comparison being made? If a distinction is made on the basis of the laws of nature or God's designed order, it is an apple/orange comparison and should be deemed legitimate. To pervert such a comparison into an apple/apple comparison and claim violation of equality principles is a false comparison and a stronghold that must be exposed and rejected.

If the Supreme Court of Vermont would have considered the nature of the distinction between homosexual couples and heterosexual couples for purposes of marriage, it would seem self-evident that the "discrimination" was not only appropriate, but also necessary. How many additional legal situations can you think of that involve the stronghold of comparison?

The Strongholds of Pride and Selfish Ambition

Most, if not all, of the previously discussed strongholds are rooted in pride and selfish ambition. Pride is fertile ground for deception and for distortion of the truth. As man considers himself to be self-sufficient, confident in his abilities, and reliant upon his reason, the "father of lies"[28] can easily manipulate attitudes and behavior. These attitudes then solidify into strongholds, blinding men from the truth and resulting in destructive, albeit sincere, philosophies.

Consider from Scripture the nature of pride from its source: Satan. Lucifer was one of the archangels, and the Bible says that

[28]John 8:44—"Ye are of your father the devil, and the lusts of your father ye will do. He was a murderer from the beginning, and abode not in the truth, because there is not truth in him. When he speaketh a lie, he speaketh of his own: for he is a liar, and the father of it."

he was the "son of the morning."[29] Then Satan reasoned that he was as great as God and purposed to be equal to God.[30] This is pride and selfish ambition to the ultimate. As a result of his pride, Lucifer was cast down upon the earth, but God did not give Satan dominion over the earth. Satan went from being a beautiful archangel in charge of one-third of the angels to being exiled in a land with no authority until Adam, through his sin, surrendered some authority to Satan.[31]

As Christians, we praise God that Jesus (the second Adam) came to live a sinless life as a man and shed His blood for the remission of sins for all those who believe. Jesus made a mockery of Satan and snatched the keys of death from him.[32] Regarding who we are "in Christ," Satan has no authority except to the degree that we knowingly or unknowingly give authority to him. Authority, or ground, is surrendered to Satan either by actions or attitudes that are opposite to loving God and our neighbor,[33] or by subtle strongholds in our lives that have blinded us to the truth of the enemy's influence.[34]

Since sin entered the world through pride, all sin has its roots in pride. As law students or lawyers, we need to constantly

[29]Isaiah 14:12—"How art thou fallen from heaven, O Lucifer, son of the morning! how art thou cut down to the ground, which didst weaken the nations!"

[30]Isaiah 14:13–14—"For thou hast said in thine heart, I will ascend into heaven, I will exalt my throne above the stars of God: I will sit also upon the mount of the congregation, in the sides of the north: I will ascend above the heights of the clouds; I will be like the most High."

[31]Revelation 12:9—"And the great dragon was cast out, that old serpent, called the Devil, and Satan, which deceiveth the whole world: he was cast out into the earth, and his angels were cast out with him." Genesis 3:4-6—"And the serpent said unto the woman, Ye shall not surely die: For God doth know that in the day ye eat thereof, then your eyes shall be opened, and ye shall be as gods, knowing good and evil. And when the woman saw that the tree was good for food, and that it was pleasant to the eyes, and a tree to be desired to make one wise, she took of the fruit thereof, and did eat, and gave also unto her husband with her; and he did eat."

[32]Colossians 2:13–15—"And you, being dead in your sins and the uncircumcision of your flesh, hath he quickened together with him, having forgiven you all trespasses; Blotting out the handwriting of ordinances that was against us, which was contrary to us, and took it out of the way, nailing it to his cross; And having spoiled principalities and powers, he made a shew of them openly, triumphing over them in it."

[33]Matthew 22:36–40—"Master, which is the great commandment in the law? Jesus said unto him, Thou shalt love the Lord thy God with all thy heart, and with all thy soul, and with all thy mind. This is the first and great commandment. And the second is like unto it, Thou shalt love thy neighbor as thyself. On these two hang all the law and the prophets."

[34]Ephesians 6:11–12—"Put on the whole armour of God, that ye may be able to stand against the wiles of the devil. For we wrestle not against flesh and blood, but against principalities, against powers, against the rulers of the darkness of this world, against spiritual wickedness in high places."

remind ourselves that we can do nothing apart from God[35] and that it is through our weaknesses that God proves Himself strong.[36] If we humble ourselves before God, He will exalt us for His glory, not ours.[37] Whether it is in the cases we read, the study aids we use, or the discussions we have, we constantly need to be alert for the manifestations of the strongholds of pride and selfish ambition. Only through humility will you experience the blessings God wants to give you during your legal studies. "By humility and the fear of the LORD are riches, and honour, and life" (Proverbs 22:4).

[35]John 15:5—"I am the vine, ye are the branches: He that abideth in me, and I in him, the same bringeth forth much fruit: for without me ye can do nothing."

[36]II Corinthians 12:9–10—"And he said unto me, My grace is sufficient for thee: for my strength is made perfect in weakness. Most gladly therefore will I rather glory in my infirmities, that the power of Christ may rest upon me. Therefore I take pleasure in infirmities, in reproaches, in necessities, in persecutions, in distresses for Christ's sake: for when I am weak, then am I strong."

[37]James 4:10—"Humble yourselves in the sight of the Lord, and he shall lift you up." I Peter 5:6—"Humble yourselves therefore under the mighty hand of God, that he may exalt you in due time."

Chapter Two

Renewing the Mind

> *I beseech you therefore, brethren, by the mercies of God, that ye present your bodies a living sacrifice, holy, acceptable unto God, which is your reasonable service. And be not conformed to this world: but be ye transformed by the renewing of your mind, that ye may prove what is that good, and acceptable, and perfect, will of God.* Romans 12:1–2

A study of the signers of the Declaration of Independence reveals that they were seekers of truth. While they may have had differences of opinion on some issues, they had the same goal of establishing a nation on a solid foundation. With deep convictions about the rightness of their cause, they pledged their lives, fortunes, and sacred honor to each other. They relied upon the Supreme Judge of the world for the rectitude of their intentions and trusted in Divine Providence for protection. They all realized the need to justify legally the separation from England upon the basis of truth, not some man-centered political philosophy. They knew that it was only the "Laws of Nature and of Nature's God" that entitled them to assume the status of a separate and equal nation.

As seekers of truth and well acquainted with the failed political systems of the past, these great men of faith boldly stated that there are some things that are "self-evident." Self-evident means that it requires no proof and that there is no need for evidence to establish the fact because it is so obvious and so unquestionable. To even question the reality of a self-evident truth would be foolishness, and anyone who challenged the veracity of such truths did not even deserve an honorable response.

As law students and lawyers, we need to be seekers and believers of truth as were our Founding Fathers. It is not enough to tear down the strongholds in legal thinking. Those strongholds must be replaced with towers of truth. Otherwise, false philosophies—seven times greater—may replace the previously held false ideas.[38]

---

[38]Luke 11:24–26—"When the unclean spirit is gone out of a man, he walketh through dry places, seeking rest; and finding none, he saith, I will return unto my house whence I came out. And when he cometh, he findeth it swept and garnished. Then goeth he, and taketh to him seven other spirits more wicked than himself; and they enter in, and dwell there: and the last state of that man is worse than the first."

Wrong paradigms need to be replaced with right ones. Deceptive legal tests and standards must be replaced with principles of justice and mercy.

At Oak Brook College of Law (OBCL) we strongly believe that many aspects of our current legal system need to be thoroughly examined and that some aspects need to be changed. If OBCL students learn and believe the same humanistic legal philosophies taught in most other law schools, there is no reason for Oak Brook College to exist. Our goal is to be a school of students and faculty committed to the pursuit of truth based upon God's created order and the reality of the kingdom of God as revealed in the Holy Scriptures. Like Solomon, we desire to have understanding hearts to know the difference between what is good and bad when it comes to the law and legal strategies.[39]

In this chapter, we will explore some towers of truth that should replace the strongholds rooted in humanism and in evolutionary philosophies. We must pursue truth from the Source of Truth, Jesus the Messiah. Just as a deer pants for water, so we should hunger and thirst after Him.[40] He is the way, the truth, and the life,[41] and all the treasures of wisdom and knowledge are hidden in Him.[42] Not only will the truth set us free,[43] but the wisdom from above will confound the worldly wise men of our day.[44] Legal strategies, insights into human relationships, and principled arguments will be the fruit of a life committed to knowing the Truth. Whether serving as legal counselors,[45] advocates,[46] or mediators,[47] our example is Jesus Christ, the righteous One. Any goal short of this is contrary to the vision and purpose of Oak Brook College.

---

[39]I Kings 3:9—"Give therefore thy servant an understanding heart to judge thy people, that I may discern between good and bad: for who is able to judge this thy so great a people?"

[40]Psalm 42:1—"As the hart panteth after the water brooks, so panteth my soul after thee, O God."

[41]John 14:6—"Jesus saith unto him, I am the way, the truth, and the life: no man cometh unto the Father, but by me."

[42]Colossians 2:3—"In whom are hid all the treasures of wisdom and knowledge."

[43]John 8:31–32—"Then said Jesus to those Jews which believed on him, If ye continue in my word, then are ye my disciples indeed; And ye shall know the truth, and the truth shall make you free."

[44]I Corinthians 1:27—"But God hath chosen the foolish things of the world to confound the wise; and God hath chosen the weak things of the world to confound the things which are mighty."

[45]Isaiah 9:6—"For unto us a child is born, unto us a son is given: and the government shall be upon his shoulder: and his name shall be called Wonderful, Counsellor, The mighty God, The everlasting Father, The Prince of Peace."

[46]I John 2:1—"My little children, these things write I unto you, that ye sin not. And if any man sin, we have an advocate with the Father, Jesus Christ the righteous."

[47]I Timothy 2:5—"For there is one God, and one mediator between God and men, the man Christ Jesus."

This chapter requires you to consider several areas of law and legal study that need renewal. Perhaps it would be better to say that you will be considering foundational principles upon which to build towers of truth. Over time, we inevitably conform to some of the world's ways of thinking, oftentimes unconsciously. This is certainly true of those who had little or no Biblical training during their years of formal education. As with other areas in our lives, the way we think about law and about our judicial system may need to be "taken captive" and examined. For some it will be a new process; for others it will be part of renewing the mind.

Approach to Legal Education

Oak Brook College is unique for several reasons. Its student body consists mostly of home-educated students who desire to be trained as professional lawyers. Its faculty consists of practicing lawyers committed to helping students gain the academic and practical skills necessary to be profitable legal servants. Its curriculum is via distance learning, and it requires a student to be self-disciplined and determined to complete it successfully. This is not a program for the fainthearted or uncommitted. It requires a student to have a "pioneer" spirit and be willing to face opposition and scorn for the methods used and the principles taught.

Oak Brook College's approach to legal education is certainly not the contemporary way nor is it the easiest way, but it is intended to be a principled way based upon a historical approach to education. In fact, it is an attempt to teach law in a way similar to the approach used before the late nineteenth century. Legal education took a dramatic shift in the late 1800s and early 1900s as a result of the efforts by some to view law as a science. Darwinian philosophy emerged in law schools, primarily through the efforts of Christopher Columbus Langdell at the Harvard Law School. Greatly influenced by evolutionary teachings, Langdell set out to change the paradigm of legal education by infusing scientific methodology into the study of law. He said that "the law library was a lawyer's laboratory" and that law was derived from the cases.

Along with the influence of scientific methodology, the Socratic method of teaching gained popularity in law schools. It was believed, and still is by most professors, that the Socratic method of asking a series of provocative questions on a particular issue is the best way to teach law students to "think like a lawyer." It may help students learn to think, but depending on the worldview of the professor, it can also intimidate law students into abandoning their "irrational" moral views and adopting a type of "scientific" approach to legal issues that excludes any absolutes or foundational principles of law. If a student views the moral foundations of law as irrelevant, a student can easily adopt a perspective that the only goal in practicing law is "winning." Such lawyers will likely make whatever arguments are expedient—even if it means compromising principle—to get what their client wants.

Clearly, lawyers need to be trained to think critically and must be able to analyze legal issues from different perspectives, but that does not mean that they need to abandon the moral base that was incorporated into the American legal system before the advent of evolutionary thought. In fact, our whole Common Law system is rooted in the moral truths and principles of justice derived from the Bible. To forsake these moral foundations would be to pull the anchor on the ship of our legal system and to allow the ship to drift according to the winds of societal influences to a destination unknown. When rooted in absolute principles of justice, lawyers can withstand the winds of passion, selfish gain, and reputation to perform the service of being counselors and advocates for justice.

Before the philosophical shift in legal education, lawyers were trained to think in terms of principles. These principles were based upon the law of nature and experience proven to be important in resolving conflicts and leading to just results. Cases were recorded to give guidance in how to apply these principles in future cases. The cases were examples of the application of these principles. They were not the source of the law, but as Blackstone said, they were "evidence of the law." Blackstone also said that a previous court decision should be respected and followed, unless it was contrary to reason or violated the law of nature.

At Oak Brook College, we take the traditional approach to legal education. Law should be taught from a principled perspective, and students should be trained to think in terms of those principles. Cases are used to illustrate the application of the principles or to raise questions as to how the principles should have been applied, but were not. Cases are not looked upon as the source of the law, but are used to demonstrate current legal reasoning and the dangers of abandoning moral absolutes in the administration of justice. As time and resources permit, Oak Brook College will work toward developing its own materials for the various courses to further implement this perspective on teaching the law and training students to think according to the wisdom from above and not according to the wisdom of the world.

What Is Law?

If one is interested in studying law, it seems fitting that one of the first areas in which strongholds need to be torn down and towers of truth built concerns the nature and purpose of law. As was previously mentioned, there are those who view law only as an instrument of social change. To such people, the nature and purpose of law are not necessarily related to any absolute moral standards, and it certainly must be flexible enough to address current cultural changes! At the opposite end of the spectrum there are those who advocate that the only laws a nation should have are those laws of God that have not been modified or abolished by the teachings of Jesus Christ.

Our goal at Oak Brook College is to give you the perspective of law held by our Founding Fathers as revealed in seminal legal documents. Without knowing the parameters of man's ability to create law, our legal system can become "lawless." Law could become only what those in power say. Rather than being bound by the law, those in power would then become the law. A "might makes right" mentality would develop rather than the Biblical and traditional American view that "right makes might."

To discern the Founding Fathers' view of the nature and purpose of law, one needs to look at the writings of William Blackstone on the Common Law and then look to the seminal documents of this nation. William Blackstone (1723–1780) was a jurist in England whose *Commentaries on the Law of England* served as the basic text for the study of law during the early history of America. He defined law generally as "a rule of action" and said that it is "prescribed by some superior, and which the inferior is bound to obey." He immediately went on to say that it was the "Supreme Being" Who "impressed certain principles" upon His creation "from which it can never depart, and without which it would cease to be."

Man's relationship to the Creator was also made clear in Blackstone's *Commentaries*. He said, "Man, considered as a creature, must necessarily be subject to the laws of his Creator, for he is entirely a dependent being." Consequently, "as man depends absolutely upon his Maker for everything, it is necessary that he should in all points conform to his Maker's will. This will of his Maker is called the law of Nature."

The law of nature sets the parameter for our legal and governmental system. Blackstone said that the law of nature was "superior in obligation to any other" and "binding over all the globe, in all countries, and at all times." From this perspective, it is easy to see why Blackstone concluded that "no human laws are of any validity if contrary to this [law of nature]."

According to Blackstone, the law of nature was discovered by man's reason, but because man's reason is "corrupt, and his understanding full of ignorance and error," God in His mercy "hath been pleased, at sundry times and in diverse manners, to discover and enforce its laws by an immediate and direct revelation. The doctrines thus delivered we call the revealed or divine law, and they are to be found only in the Holy Scriptures." Blackstone said that upon the law of nature and the law of revelation "depend all human laws; that is to say, no human laws should be suffered to contradict these."

In addition to the law of nature and the law of revelation, Blackstone also discussed municipal law. This was law made by man to govern the affairs of man in a civil society. Specifically, he defined municipal law as a "rule of civil conduct prescribed by the supreme power in a state commanding what is right and prohibiting what is wrong." This definition is derived from Romans 13 and I Peter 2,[48] which indicate that the role of civil government is to punish those who do wrong and to praise those who do good. The municipal law must be consistent with God's will (the law of nature), but it can include rules that man deems to be in the best interest of society. Because God has not dictated a specific commandment in all areas of life, man has the liberty to establish rules and regulations within the boundaries of the law of nature.

Blackstone not only discussed the types of law, but he also discussed the characteristics or nature of law. Remember, Blackstone said that law was a rule of action. All law (whether it be the law of nature, law of revelation, or municipal law) has this characteristic. By a "rule of action," Blackstone meant that it is not a "transient sudden order from a superior to or concerning a particular person; but something permanent, uniform and universal." By "permanent" he meant fixed as to time, that is, it does not change over time without the supreme authority taking specific steps to change it. A rule can be contrasted to counsel or advice. A rule is also not a compact or a covenant. Counsel or advice is not mandatory, and a covenant is only between a limited number of parties. A rule is a mandate that everyone in a particular jurisdiction must follow.

---

[48]Romans 13:3–4—"For rulers are not a terror to good works, but to the evil. Wilt thou then not be afraid of the power? do that which is good, and thou shalt have praise of the same: For he is the minister of God to thee for good. But if thou do that which is evil, be afraid; for he beareth not the sword in vain: for he is the minister of God, a revenger to execute wrath upon him that doeth evil." I Peter 2:14—"Or unto governors, as unto them that are sent by him for the punishment of evildoers, and for the praise of them that do well."

Secondly, a rule must be uniform as to person or situation, that is, the law must be applied equally upon all people. This is mandated by the Biblical principle of impartiality. God said that showing partiality in judgment perverts justice,[49] and if a law does not apply to everyone equally, partiality is shown. Everyone within a jurisdiction subject to a law should have equal protection under the law and must be equally subject to the law.

Finally, the rule must be universal as to place. This means that the law must be binding everywhere within a given jurisdiction and that the rule is not relative as to place. The same rule must apply in one part of the jurisdiction as in another. Again, this principle is to prevent the showing of partiality. Absent good reason for a different rule in a different location, the law applies everywhere.

In summary, law is a rule of action imposed by an authority upon those under authority commanding what is right and prohibiting what is wrong. A law is permanent as to time, uniformly applied to all people and universally applied in all locations within a jurisdiction.

This was the legal view of law in England, but was it the view in the American colonies? One must realize that the colonies were under English law for over 150 years before the Declaration of Independence, and that the Common Law of England was the basis for any colonial law prior to the Declaration. Within the Declaration itself, we see evidence that the Biblical view of law not only still existed, but that it was the very legal foundation for the separation from England.

In the Declaration we read, "When in the course of human events, it becomes necessary for one people to dissolve the political bands which have connected them with another, and to assume among the Powers of the earth, the separate and equal station to which the Laws of Nature and of Nature's God entitle them. . . ." By these words, the signers of the Declaration were referring to the same law of nature Blackstone described, as well as the law of revelation. "Laws of Nature's God" was another way of referring to God's Law. Therefore, we know that the Founders had a legal mind-set and believed that man's law must be in accordance with the law of nature for it to be valid. Certainly, the bold and dangerous move to legally declare independence from England required a legal justification consistent with the Common Law of England.

[49]Proverbs 24:23—"These things also belong to the wise. It is not good to have respect of persons in judgment." Leviticus 19:15—"Ye shall do no unrighteousness in judgment: thou shalt not respect the person of the poor, nor honor the person of the mighty: but in righteousness shalt thou judge thy neighbor."

In addition to the seminal documents of this nation, early American legal scholars confirmed that Blackstone's description of the law continued to be the legal parameter for our nation. Over one hundred years later, James Kent, the Blackstone of American law, wrote in his *Commentaries*,

> It would be improper to separate this law (positive law) entirely from natural jurisprudence and not to consider it as deriving much of its force and dignity from the same principles of right reason, the same views of the nature and constitution of man, and the same sanction of divine revelation as those from which the science of morality is deduced. There is a natural and a positive law of nations. By the former, every state in its relations with other states is bound to conduct itself with justice, good faith, and benevolence. . . .

In an 1857 treatise used as a standard textbook for law students, Theodore Sedgwick wrote this:

> Man, in whatever situation he may be placed, finds himself under the control of rules of action emanating from an authority to which he is compelled to bow—in other words, of LAW. The moment that he comes into existence, he is the subject of the will of God, as declared in what we term the laws of nature.

If this was the definition of law that was enforced during the early history of our country, what has happened? The answer can only be that man-centered philosophies gradually influenced those in positions of legal influence, namely law teachers. Their students became the next judges and legislators and reinforced the deceptive legal paradigm that man is the only source of law in a nation. In their view, any references to God as Creator and to the law of nature are in the realm of religion and have no part in a secular legal or governmental system.

The strongholds in this area of the nature and purpose of law were not erected overnight. Neither will they be torn down without much opposition, but the first step is to have a renewed mind about what law really is. Law is a rule of action that establishes the standard of civil conduct to which every person must either conform or experience consequences for violating. All human law must be consistent with God's created order (law of nature) and with His ordained authority structures revealed in the Bible (law of revelation).

From a Biblical view, people must conform their actions to the law. The law is not necessarily to be a reflection of the people's current moral views. Our Founding Fathers held the Biblical view; however, many contemporary legal scholars, judges, and legislators believe that the law should be a reflection of the people's current moral views. Unfortunately, legal education has been infiltrated with the latter philosophy for well over seventy-five years. If this were not the case, we would never have state supreme courts mandating that sodomite couples be given the same right to marry as heterosexual couples, and we would never have the Supreme Court elevating a woman's "privacy rights" over the life of an unborn human being. May God have mercy upon us as a nation!

God-Ordained Jurisdictions

The nature and purpose of law deals with the prescriptive, i.e., what should be. The law should establish the standard to which man is to conform his actions. If one violates the law, there must be consequences, so that others will be "trained" to obey the law. This is necessary to have civil order, and civil order is necessary so that the church, without restraint, can preach the Gospel.[50] But with every legal or political issue, what is "right or wrong" is only the first question that must be asked. The second—and just as important—question is, Who has the legitimate authority to respond to the problem or to do something about the violation of the law?

Just as God's will is the law of nature and all human laws must conform to the law of nature to be valid, God has also ordained who is to have authority to legislate, to judge, and to execute the law. God has established, as part of His law of nature, different jurisdictions or structures of authority to "govern" in certain areas of life. God has ordained that there be civil authority, church authority, family authority and, of course, self authority. As individuals, we are accountable to God for actions,[51] thoughts,[52] and words,[53] but we may also be

[50]I Timothy 2:1—"I exhort therefore, that, first of all, supplications, prayers, intercessions, and giving of thanks, be made for all men; For kings, and for all that are in authority; that we may lead a quiet and peaceable life in all godliness and honesty."

[51]Romans 2:6—"Who will render to every man according to his deeds." I Corinthians 3:13—"Every man's work shall be made manifest: for the day shall declare it, because it shall be revealed by fire; and the fire shall try every man's work of what sort it is."

[52]Matthew 15:19—"For out of the heart proceed evil thoughts, murders, adulteries, fornications, thefts, false witness, blasphemies." I Corinthians 3:20—"And again, The Lord knoweth the thoughts of the wise, that they are vain." Psalm 139:23–24—"Search me, O God, and know my heart: try me, and know my thoughts: And see if there be any wicked way in me, and lead me in the way everlasting."

[53]Matthew 12:36–37—"But I say unto you, That every idle word that men shall speak, they shall give account thereof in the day of judgment. For by thy words thou shalt be justified, and by the words thou shalt be condemned."

accountable to other God-ordained authorities in certain ways. The following is a brief description of the God-ordained jurisdictions.

Self-Government

The Scriptures clearly reveal that God ordained different jurisdictions to govern different areas of life. To understand the nature of these jurisdictions, one needs to begin with Creation. When God created man, He told Adam that he could eat of every tree in the garden, except of the tree of the knowledge of good and evil. When God imposed the law upon Adam, it was for man's benefit, as all law should be, but man was going to have to exercise self-control (self-government) to obey the command. Adam and Eve, by their reason and observation, rationalized away the importance of obedience and made a decision to follow their thoughts and desires rather than the will of God.

God also warned Cain of the temptation that would confront him and told Cain that "sin lieth at the door" but that Cain needed to "rule over" it.[54] Cain also failed to act according to God's command and committed murder. Consequently, God ruled that Cain would be a "fugitive and a vagabond"[55] but that no man would have authority over Cain to put him to death.[56] God had not yet granted any man the authority to execute judgment of death or physical punishment over someone else as a consequence of his or her actions. It was not until after the flood that God gave man the authority to judge and sanction other men for violating the laws of nature.[57]

Family

Another jurisdiction God created at the time of Creation was the jurisdiction of the family. God created male and female and gave them, as husband and wife, certain authority. God said, "Be fruitful, and multiply, and replenish the earth, and subdue it: and have dominion over the fish of the sea, and over the fowl of the air, and over every living thing that moveth upon the earth" (Genesis 1:28). God ordained that only a male and a female in a lifelong covenantal relationship[58] had the authority and the duty to bear children—to be fruitful and multiply.

---

[54]Genesis 4:7—"If thou doest well, shalt thou not be accepted? and if thou doest not well, sin lieth at the door. And unto thee shall be his desire, and thou shalt rule over him."

[55]Genesis 4:12—"When thou tillest the ground, it shall not henceforth yield unto thee her strength; a fugitive and a vagabond shalt thou be in the earth."

[56]Genesis 4:15—"And the LORD said unto him, Therefore whosoever slayeth Cain, vengeance shall be taken on him sevenfold. And the LORD set a mark upon Cain, lest any finding him should kill him."

[57]Genesis 9:6—"Whoso sheddeth man's blood, by man shall his blood be shed: for in the image of God made he man."

[58]Genesis 2:24—"Therefore shall a man leave his father and mother, and shall cleave unto his wife: and they shall be one flesh."

Within the parents' authority to bear children also comes the duty to train and educate them. Children are to listen to the instruction of their parents and honor them.[59] God ordained the rod of correction to be the means of enforcing the authority of the parents for young children, within the commitment to love and to nurture them in the admonition of the Lord.[60] So when it comes to family matters, the law is to be set based upon God's Word, and the enforcement and sanction of that law is also to be implemented by the family in the context of love as commanded by God.

In Genesis 1:28, commonly called the dominion mandate, God was also saying that the authority over property was a stewardship authority to be administered through the family. This is the Biblical basis for the concept of private property and free enterprise with respect to property. This is not to say that only families are involved in these areas, but it does mean that the source of the authority comes from God to and through the family. When one considers the origins of most private industries, including agriculture, science, and medicine, the dominion mandate is the source of their authority to exist.

Civil Government

As wickedness increased in the land, the people's thoughts were continually on evil, and God regretted that He had made man on the earth. With no civil authority to be God's instruments of wrath upon evildoers, God decided that it was necessary to destroy all mankind. Only Noah found favor in God's eyes, and it was through him that God planned to replenish the human race.[61]

Things were different after the flood: the landmasses were changed; God put the fear of man into all the animals; and God ordained an authority to remind people, through sanction, of His

---

[59]Ephesians 6:1–3—"Children, obey your parents in the Lord: for this is right. Honour thy father and mother; which is the first commandment with promise; That it may be well with thee, and thou mayest live long on the earth." Colossians 3:20—"Children, obey your parents in all things: for this is well pleasing unto the Lord."

[60]Colossians 3:21—"Fathers, provoke not your children to anger, lest they be discouraged." Ephesians 6:4—"And, ye fathers, provoke not your children to wrath: but bring them up in the nurture and admonition of the Lord." James 1:20—"For the wrath of man worketh not the righteousness of God." Proverbs 13:24—"He that spareth his rod hateth his son: but he that loveth him chasteneth him betimes." Proverbs 22:15—"Foolishness is bound in the heart of a child; but the rod of correction shall drive it far from him."

[61]Genesis 6:5–8—"And God saw that the wickedness of man was great in the earth, and that every imagination of the thoughts of his heart was only evil continually. And it repented the LORD that he had made man on the earth, and it grieved him at his heart. And the LORD said, I will destroy man whom I have created from the face of the earth; both man, and beast, and the creeping thing, and the fowls of the air; for it repenteth me that I have made them. But Noah found grace in the eyes of the LORD."

law of nature.[62] No longer would people be allowed to ignore the fact that God created man in His image. No longer could a person take another person's life without consequences that were administered by a God-ordained authority.

The Apostle Paul clarified the nature of civil authority in his letter to the Romans. In chapter 12, Paul made it very clear that one's only authority, as an individual, is to love. We are to live at peace with one another and not repay evil with evil. We should bless those who persecute us, and we are not to execute vengeance upon those that hurt us, because God says, "Vengeance is mine."[63]

In Romans 13, Paul tells us that every authority that exists, whether it is family, church, or civil, is ordained of God. While Paul was speaking specifically about civil rulers in this context, the same truth applies to the family and the church. The Greek word *exousia*, translated as *powers*, is probably better understood to mean "authorities." In light of this, Romans 13:1–2 could read as follows: "Let every soul be subject unto the higher authorities. For there is no authority but of God: the authorities that be are ordained of God. Whosoever therefore resisteth the authority, resisteth the ordinance of God: and they that resist shall receive to themselves damnation."

With respect to civil authority, Jesus confirmed that no ruler has authority unless God gives it to him. In John 19:11, Jesus responded to Pilate's question, "Knowest thou not that I have power to crucify thee," by saying, "Thou couldest have no power at all against me, except it were given thee from above: therefore he that delivered me unto thee hath the greater sin."

After establishing that all authority comes from God, Paul explains the purpose of civil government: to punish the evildoer. A person in a position of civil authority is a "minister of God, a revenger to execute wrath upon him that *doeth* evil." Significantly, Paul did not say "*think* evil." This is because our thoughts and the motives of our hearts are solely within God's authority to judge. The Scriptures make it very clear that He will judge our hearts and thoughts.[64] Therefore,

---

[62]Genesis 9:2, 5–6—"And the fear of you and the dread of you shall be upon every beast of the earth, and upon every fowl of the air, upon all that moveth upon the earth, and upon all the fishes of the sea; into your hand are they delivered. . . . And surely your blood of your lives will I require; at the hand of every beast will I require it, and at the hand of man; at the hand of every man's brother will I require the life of man. Whoso sheddeth man's blood, by man shall his blood be shed: for in the image of God made he man."

[63]Romans 12:19—"Dearly beloved, avenge not yourselves, but rather give place unto wrath: for it is written, Vengeance is mine; I will repay, saith the Lord."

[64]Proverbs 17:3—"The fining pot is for silver, and the furnace for gold: but the LORD trieth the hearts." Psalm 26:2—"Examine me, O LORD, and prove me; try my reins and my heart." Jeremiah 17:10—"I the LORD search the heart, I try the reins, even to give every man according to his ways, and according to the fruit of his doings."

the civil government's jurisdiction is limited to actions. While words and motives are often associated with actions and must be considered as evidences of wrong actions, only deeds directly or indirectly contrary to the law of nature are subject to the legislation, judgment, and execution of civil government.

Yet not all actions are subject to the civil government. Only those actions that involve civil conduct are within the civil government's jurisdiction. Jesus said, "Render therefore unto Caesar the things which be Caesar's and unto God the things which be God's" (Luke 20:25). This was not only a statement concerning the difference between the kingdom of God and man's earthly systems. It was also a statement of jurisdiction distinguishing between those duties one owes to God and those duties one owes to the civil government. That is why the key question to determine in which jurisdiction a particular activity belongs is, To whom do you owe the duty? If it is owed only to God, it is in the jurisdiction of self-government or the church; if it is owed to the family, the family authority governs; if the activity involves civil conduct related to maintaining and preserving civil order, the civil rulers are in authority regarding that matter.

The perspective of God-ordained jurisdictions is one that was held by our Founders. For example, the Bill of Rights of the Virginia Constitution contains this language: "That religion or the duty we owe to our Creator, and the manner of discharging it, can be directed only by reason and conviction, not by force or violence; and therefore, all men are equally entitled to the free exercise of religion, according to the dictates of conscience." If the duty is owed only to God, then it is not within the jurisdiction of the civil government. In fact, James Madison said that the duty to God (religion) is "wholly exempt from its [civil government's] cognizance."[65]

Church

The other authority that God clearly ordained is the church, meaning the New Testament church that Christ instituted before He ascended into Heaven. Jesus said, "All power [authority] is given unto me in heaven and in earth. Go ye therefore, and teach all nations, baptizing them in the name of the Father, and of the Son, and of the Holy Ghost. Teaching them to observe all things whatsoever I have commanded you: and, lo, I am with you alway, even unto the end of the world" (Matthew 28:18–20). In this pronouncement, Jesus was saying that all authority (including family and civil authority) was under Him but that He was now delegating to believers the

[65]James Madison, *Memorial and Remonstrance Against Religious Assessments (1785).*

authority to preach and to teach about the kingdom of God. At this time, Jesus did not change the family jurisdiction or the civil authority (even though He had the authority to do so). Therefore, until Jesus returns, the civil jurisdiction remains God-ordained, and the form remains man-instituted. The family remains the legitimate authority for dominion, and the church has the authority over the association of believers to "teach all nations."

It is interesting to note that the Great Commission was cited in the colonial charters as the justification for coming to another land to establish a social and political structure. For example, the Charter of Virginia stated:

> We, greatly commending, and graciously accepting of, their Desires for the Furtherance of so noble a Work, which may, by the Providence of Almighty God, hereafter tend to the Glory of his Divine Majesty, in propagating of *Christian* Religion to such People, as yet live in Darkness and miserable Ignorance of the true Knowledge and Worship of God, and may in time bring the Infidels and Savages, living in those parts, to human Civility, and to a settled and quiet Government: DO, by these our Letters Patents, graciously accept of, and agree to, their humble and well-intended Desires.

Because the Great Commission is not limited to geographic or political boundaries, every believer has the God-ordained authority and duty to make disciples of Christ. This authority necessarily includes the authority to build homes and establish a community for that purpose. Whether or not preaching the Gospel of Jesus Christ was the motivation of all who came to the New World is certainly subject to debate, but the legal documents clearly demonstrate that it was the stated legal reason.

Foundations of Common Law Courses

In the first year of law school, you study three Common Law courses in addition to Legal Research and Writing: Torts, Contracts, and Criminal Law. These courses are based upon the principles developed in the Common Law of England. As was mentioned, these principles are consistent with the law of nature and were utilized in resolving conflicts in a way that led to just results. Early in your study of these courses, it is important to understand the historical meaning of the Common Law and its Biblical foundations.

Blackstone said that the Common Law included not only general customs but also the particular customs of certain parts of the kingdom, and likewise those particular laws that are by custom observed only in certain courts and jurisdictions. In response to the question, "How are these customs or maxims to be known, and by whom is their validity to be determined," Blackstone stated, "The answer is by the judges in the several courts of justice." He went on to say that the judges were the "depositories of the laws, the living oracles, who must decide in all cases of doubt, and who are bound by an oath to decide according to the law of the land."

For these reasons, Blackstone said judicial opinions were considered "evidence of what is the Common Law," but it was clear that "the law and the opinion of the judge are not always convertible terms, one and the same thing; since it sometimes may happen that the judge may mistake the law." Although the Common Law was court-articulated law, it was not court-made law. It was with this understanding that previous court decisions were followed unless "the former determination is most evidently contrary to reason; much more, if it be clearly contrary to Divine law. For if it be found that the former decision is manifestly absurd or unjust, it is declared not that such a sentence was bad law, but that it was not law."[66]

Based on this explanation of why the role of a judge was to articulate the Common Law, it is clear that judges were not the sources of law, but only the expounders of it. Any decision or opinion written by a judge was within the parameters of the law of nature and the revealed law. Within this context, the law of torts, contracts, and criminal law was developed and established.

The principles of law that you will study in these courses are derived from many years of application. The rules can be memorized and easily stated, but the application of these rules is often the challenge. Factual distinctions and differences in today's culture require a thorough understanding of the underlying principles of the rules before a just result can be reached in a current case. This is one reason why it is so important to read and study the cases assigned. The discipline of studying cases will help teach you legal reasoning. You will read examples of sound reasoning and correct application of the principles, but you will also read perversions of justice when personal interests or false premises are determinative in a decision. Legal reasoning skills are developed **only** by analyzing and briefing cases, thinking up hypothetical situations, applying the principles, writing out responses to essay questions, and completing other writing projects.

---

[66]Quotes from I W. BLACKSTONE, COMMENTARIES *68–71.

Common Law courses are different from Code courses such as the Uniform Commercial Code or Federal Income Tax. The former involves logical reasoning to apply principles of law to a current situation. The latter requires one to develop skill in statutory interpretation and in the application of specific Code provisions to the facts. With both types of courses, deductive reasoning is important, but probably more so with the Common Law courses. Deductive reasoning starts with a general proposition applied to a specific situation. It often involves major and minor premises to reach a conclusion. This is called a syllogism.

Inductive reasoning is arriving at a general conclusion based upon the accumulation of specific facts or observations. It is going from the specific to the general. Because the Common Law developed over time and the law was articulated in court opinions, some think that the Common Law was derived from cases. This is not true. Cases were just evidence or applications of the Common Law. Sometimes the principles previously articulated in prior court opinions were extended to a new fact pattern and resulted in a new application of the principles, but the new court opinion was not the source of the law, it was only the application of the law. Yet, because the new application of principles became precedent for future cases, it is understandable why some would loosely say that court decisions "created" new law. In this manner, principles of tort, contract, and criminal law developed over time, and the "law" in each of these areas is articulated in cases, not in statutes or written codes.

As was stated, the Common Law was based upon the law of nature and God's revealed law. As you proceed in your study of the three first-year Common Law courses, it is useful to examine the Biblical principles that are the foundations of each of these courses. All of the Common Law courses you will study during your first year presuppose that man is created in the image of God, and therefore, is of great value. From this premise are derived the rights to life, liberty, and the pursuit of happiness. Our Declaration of Independence states that it is these unalienable rights that our civil government has a duty to protect.[67] These rights are secured, in part, by laws that prohibit certain types of behavior and that establish principles by which disputes between individuals can be resolved.

---

[67]Declaration of Independence—"We hold these truths to be self-evident, that all Men are created equal, that they are endowed by their Creator with certain unalienable Rights, that among these are Life, Liberty, and the Pursuit of Happiness—That to secure these Rights, Governments are instituted among Men, deriving their just Powers from the Consent of the Governed . . . ."

Law that prohibits certain types of behavior is the focus of criminal law; law that establishes principles by which disputes between individuals can be resolved is the focus of both contract and tort law.

Contracts

Part of the right to the pursuit of happiness is the liberty to enter into relationships with others for common purposes. This includes the right to contract with another for economic gain, the right to acquire property, and the right to perform or receive services. "Contracts" is the law that governs commitments and promises between individuals, but not all promises. If there is a dispute between parties, only promises that are civilly enforceable will be reviewed by a court. Civilly enforceable promises are those promises made between people who were motivated by some gain they would receive as a result of the promise. That value is called *consideration*, and it must be of legal value, not just moral value.

Courts will also enforce promises that reasonably cause the promisee to rely (to his detriment) upon the promise. The law will not allow someone to induce another to act to his detriment without providing some type of remedy to the injured party. While we are morally accountable to God for all our promises,[68] only promises supported by consideration or detrimental reliance will be enforceable by a civil court.

We do not have the law of contracts simply because society thinks it is a good idea for people to keep their legal promises. The law of contracts is rooted in the fact that man is created in God's image. Part of that image is the ability to create, not *ex nihilo* as God did, but by using raw materials, and by using our words. Man can create and destroy relationships by his words.[69] Because God's Word is true and He performs His Word,[70] we—being created in His image—should also be true to our word. If we do not keep our promises, we bring reproach upon God, since we are created in His image. We defame God's character and take His name in vain when we do not keep our commitments. In addition, not speaking

[68]Matthew 12:36–37—"But I say unto you, That every idle word that men shall speak, they shall give account thereof in the day of judgment. For by thy words thou shalt be justified, and by thy words thou shalt be condemned." Matthew 5:37—"But let your communication be, Yea, yea; Nay, nay: for whatsoever is more than these cometh of evil."

[69]Proverbs 18:21—"Death and life are in the power of the tongue: and they that love it shall eat the fruit thereof."

[70]Numbers 23:19—"God is not a man, that he should lie; neither the son of man, that he should repent: hath he said, and shall he not do it? or hath he spoken, and shall he not make it good?

the truth is lying, which God condemns,[71] and in a legal setting, lying constitutes bearing false witness.[72]

Therefore, the Biblical foundations of contract law stem from the fact that man is created in the image of God. Man has the liberty from God to not bind himself by his words or actions, but if he does make promises, he must keep them.[73] These concepts are called *liberty of contract* and *sanctity of promise*. If man does not keep his legal promises, he violates the law of nature and also destroys the basis for legal and economic relationships, both of which are necessary for a stable polity and economy. From this perspective, contract law involves holding people to God's standard with respect to their civilly enforceable promises. When people keep their promises, they reflect God's character and demonstrate love to their neighbors, who would be damaged if promises were not kept.

Torts

Although different from contract law in many ways, tort law is also founded on the truth that man is created in the image of God. There are many different types of tort actions, while contract law involves only an agreement and a breach. Torts include intentional torts against one's person or property, claims for damages resulting from one's negligence, and responsibility for damages caused even when no one was negligent. This is called strict liability.

If one intentionally or negligently causes injury to someone else or his property, under the Biblical principle of restitution, the injured party should be compensated. This is man's only way of making the injured person "whole" after the destruction that occurred through no fault of his own. God makes it clear that we are responsible for our actions, and if we intentionally or negligently cause injury to another, we should restore that person by paying for expenses, time, and disability. Sometimes property can be replaced, but damage to the physical body may never heal, and the injured individual may experience economic and physical limitations for

---

[71] Revelation 21:8—"But the fearful, and unbelieving, and the abominable, and murderers, and whoremongers, and sorcerers, and idolaters, and all liars, shall have their part in the lake which burneth with fire and brimstone: which is the second death."

[72] Exodus 20:16—"Thou shalt not bear false witness against thy neighbour."

[73] Ecclesiastes 5:4–5—"When thou vowest a vow unto God, defer not to pay it; for he hath no pleasure in fools: pay that which thou has vowed. Better is it that thou shouldest not vow, than that thou shouldest vow and not pay." Deuteronomy 23:21–23—"When thou shalt vow a vow unto the LORD thy God, thou shalt not slack to pay it: for the LORD thy God will surely require it of thee; and it would be sin in thee. But if thou shalt forbear to vow, it shall be no sin in thee. That which is gone out of thy lips thou shalt keep and perform; even a freewill offering, according as thou hast vowed unto the LORD thy God, which thou hast promised with thy mouth."

the rest of his life. In such situations, God requires that restitution and compensation be paid.[74]

The Biblical principle of fault is the basis for tort law. Civil responsibility to pay damages to another for injury to a person or property requires that the accused be "at fault" as defined by legal principles developed over the years. The principle of fault does not require one to pay for damages if the injury was truly an unforseeable accident.

The Biblical truth that individuals should be held responsible for the consequences of their negligent and intentional actions is also at the root of the Common Law principles of criminal law.

Criminal Law

The Biblical basis for criminal law originated with the very establishment of civil authority. When God said that if one intentionally kills a person, the perpetrator must be put to death, He established the first criminal law. God specifically said that the reason for this law was because man was created in God's image.[75] This sanction was necessary to uphold the sanctity of God's image in man and to cleanse the land from the shedding of innocent blood.[76]

Within this authority for capital punishment was also given the authority for lesser corporal punishment, such as "stripes." This form of sanction also was limited by the truth that man is created in the image of God. Forty stripes were the limit, lest the perpetrator be degraded and become vile.[77] If one examines the Scriptures carefully, it becomes clear that the main purpose for stripes and even the death penalty is not retaliation, but restoration and restitution. Criminal sanction impresses upon the perpetrator the evil he committed, it instructs the simple-minded so that they do not commit the same evil acts, and it reinforces the sanctity of human life and the unalienable rights of liberty and property.

---

[74]*See* Exodus 21–22.

[75]Genesis 9:6—"Whoso sheddeth man's blood, by man shall his blood be shed: for in the image of God made he man."

[76]Numbers 35:31, 33—"Moreover ye shall take no satisfaction for the life of a murderer, which is guilty of death: but he shall be surely put to death. . . . So ye shall not pollute the land wherein ye are: for blood it defileth the land: and the land cannot be cleansed of the blood that is shed therein, but by the blood of him that shed it." Deuteronomy 19:11–13—"But if any man hate his neighbour, and lie in wait for him, and rise up against him, and smite him mortally that he die, and fleeth into one of these cities: Then the elders of his city shall send and fetch him thence, and deliver him into the hand of the avenger of blood, that he may die. Thine eye shall not pity him, but thou shalt put away the guilt of innocent blood from Israel, that it may go well with thee."

[77]Deuteronomy 25:3—"Forty stripes he may give him, and not exceed: lest, if he should exceed, and beat him above these with many stripes, then thy brother should seem vile unto thee."

A specific example of this restorative purpose is the *lex talionis*, commonly referred to as the "eye for eye, tooth for tooth" principle.[78] The context of these verses shows that the *lex talionis* cannot be interpreted literally. Rather, it is a principle of proportionality with respect to the appropriate sanction for a transgression. The *lex talionis* takes into consideration the mental state of the perpetrator and the nature of the wrong done. The sanction inflicted upon an evildoer must be proportional to the harm done and to the blameworthiness of the perpetrator. A tooth is not literally taken for a tooth, but the sanction is commensurate with the harm done.

Principle of Impartiality

A principle that is very important in criminal law, as well as in all areas of law, is the command to not show partiality.[79] Since all people are created in the image of God, all people should be accountable to the same standard. It is improper to judge one person differently from another because of economic status, appearance, or friendship. Showing partiality perverts judgment because the basis of the judgment becomes something other than facts and truth. Justice is the administration of the truth, but partiality is the granting of special privileges. Even Jesus warned against judging by appearances,[80] and James rebuked the church for showing favoritism within its assembly.[81]

The principle of impartiality should not be confused with the legitimate variation that can occur in criminal sanctions. Unless there is a mandatory sentence for a crime, judges have the discretion in sentencing a convicted defendant. The judge will consider several factors in deciding the appropriate sanction, but it must be within

---

[78]Exodus 21:23–27—"And if any mischief follow, then thou shalt give life for life, Eye for eye, tooth for tooth, hand for hand, foot for foot, Burning for burning, wound for wound, stripe for stripe. And if a man smite the eye of his servant, or the eye of his maid, that it perish; he shall let him go free for his eye's sake. And if he smite out his manservant's tooth, or his maidservant's tooth; he shall let him go free for his tooth's sake." See also Deuteronomy 19:21 and Leviticus 24:17–21.

[79]Leviticus 19:15—"Ye shall do no unrighteousness in judgment: thou shalt not respect the person of the poor, nor honour the person of the mighty: but in righteousness shalt thou judge thy neighbour." Deuteronomy 16:19—"Thou shalt not wrest judgment; thou shalt not respect persons, neither take a gift: for a gift doth blind the eyes of the wise, and pervert the words of the righteous." Proverbs 24:23—"These things also belong to the wise. It is not good to have respect of persons in judgment."

[80]John 7:24—"Judge not according to the appearance, but judge righteous judgment."

[81]James 2:2–4—"For if there come unto your assembly a man with a gold ring, in goodly apparel, and there come in also a poor man in vile raiment; And ye have respect to him that weareth the gay clothing, and say unto him, Sit thou here in a good place; and say to the poor, Stand thou there, or sit here under my footstool: Are ye not then partial in yourselves, and are become judges of evil thoughts?"

the range allowed by law. This is not showing partiality, because the judgment of guilt or innocence has already been made, presumably upon the evidence and law, without any regard for the economic, social, or political status of the defendant.

If mercy is granted before there is a judgment of guilt, partiality is shown and justice perverted. There can be no mercy until there has been a judgment as to whether the defendant has violated the standard of behavior to which all must conform. That judgment could be a voluntary self-judgment—as when a defendant confesses to a crime and pleads guilty—or an involuntary judgment, as when there is a trial and the defendant is adjudged guilty beyond a reasonable doubt. The point is that the principle of impartiality is most important at the judgment stage. Variation of sentences among defendants who have committed the same type of crime is permissible and very appropriate when mercy is warranted, because of complete repentance and restitution, or for other reasons.

The purpose of God's Law is to bring people to repentance and to the Source of judgment and mercy—Jesus Christ.[82] As ministers of God to execute wrath upon those that do evil, government leaders—through criminal law—can be used by God to fulfill a similar role. When one is confronted with the consequences of breaking the law, he may realize his inability to save himself from the lawful consequences of his actions. That realization can bring him to repentance and cause him to plead for mercy from the court. It can also cause one to realize his need for an eternal Savior. While there still must be some sanction to fulfill the justice element of the criminal law on earth, a repentant defendant can experience the mercy of Christ with respect to his eternal destiny, even at the point of death.[83]

Because all of these principles regard sanctions for infringing upon one's unalienable right to life, it is necessary to keep them before our eyes. Man has great value, and no one has the authority to take another person's life or inflict injury upon another without suffering consequences. If there were no consequences, God's image in man would be ignored, and man would be treated as if he had no more value than animals. Although God did create the animals, they do not bear His image as man does.

There are also crimes against man's liberty and property. These crimes also involve infringements upon the God-given unalienable

---

[82]Galatians 3:24—"Wherefore the law was our schoolmaster to bring us unto Christ, that we might be justified by faith."

[83]Luke 23:42–43—"And he said unto Jesus, Lord, remember me when thou comest into thy kingdom. And Jesus said unto him, Verily I say unto thee, Today shalt thou be with me in paradise."

rights each of us has as a human being. Freedom within the law of nature involves a duty we have to God to use our liberty in ways that are good. For someone to restrict our freedom inhibits the fulfillment of our duty to God, and therefore, it is a violation of our right of freedom among men.

God also established that man has a stewardship duty with respect to property entrusted to him. We really do not "own" our private property. We have a type of ownership in that, as among other men, we have the superior right, but God is the One who really owns it.[84] If someone takes or destroys our property, that person prevents us from fulfilling our stewardship duty to God with respect to that property. Such an action infringes upon our unalienable right to property and is indirectly an assault against God and His ordained order.

Therefore, whether the crime involves a person or a person's property, a criminal act infringes upon one's unalienable right to life, liberty, or property. There are other crimes that are statutory in nature, that is, they are criminal only because they violate a code (e.g., speed laws). However, all crimes involving person or property are based upon the Biblical truth that man is created in God's image. If someone violates that image in man or infringes upon one's duty to God with respect to life, liberty, or property, you have what has been called a "Common Law" crime, such as murder, rape, burglary, assault, or battery.

If you call the authority that God gave man in Genesis 1:26–28 the "dominion authority," you could say that a Common Law crime occurs when someone infringes upon or violates the dominion authority that another person has. With that dominion authority also comes the responsibility or duty before God to be a faithful steward of the objects of the authority. For this authority, man is directly accountable to God and has an unalienable right among men to fulfill that authority as he deems best. Interference with or deprivation of that dominion authority is a violation of one's unalienable rights and must not go unpunished.

So whether it is tort law, contracts, or criminal law, the purpose is to uphold the dignity and character of God in us, as His image bearers, and to act consistently with His created order with respect to property ownership, human life, and liberty.

---

[84]Psalm 24:1–2—"The earth is the LORD'S, and the fulness thereof; the world, and they that dwell therein. For he hath founded it upon the seas, and established it upon the floods."

CHAPTER THREE

PUTTING ON THE CHARACTER OF CHRIST

And we know that all things work together for good to them that love God, to them who are the called according to his purpose. For whom he did foreknow, he also did predestinate to be conformed to the image of his Son, that he might be the firstborn among many brethren. Romans 8:28–29

The character of Jesus Christ is perfection. He manifested to the world the fullness of the fruit of the Holy Spirit in love, joy, peace, patience, gentleness, goodness, faithfulness, meekness, and self-control. He is love, and He demonstrated all the aspects of love described in I Corinthians 13. Can we demonstrate the same character of Christ? Can we love as He did? Can we be patient as He was patient? Can we be as self-controlled as He was self-controlled? The answer is simply "no." We, in ourselves, cannot do what Jesus did, because we are weakened by our flesh and our sinful desires.

The only real way to live the Christian life and to demonstrate the character of Christ is to die. We have to surrender ourselves, our desires, our ambitions, and even our physical needs to the Lordship of Jesus Christ. Jesus said, "Whosoever will come after me, let him deny himself, and take up his cross, and follow me. For whosoever will save his life shall lose it; but whosoever shall lose his life for my sake and the gospel's, the same shall save it" (Mark 8:34–35). The only way to receive the power to live the Christian life is to allow God to live through us. This means that we must decrease and He must increase.[85] When we are empty vessels, Jesus is able to live through us and do many mighty works that bring glory to the Father.[86]

Paul certainly understood and experienced the life that comes through death to self. The sixth, seventh, and eighth chapters of the Book of Romans speak of the victory over sin that one experiences as one identifies with the crucifixion of Christ and the power of the life in the Holy Spirit, Who enables us to "mortify the deeds of the body."[87]

---

[85]John 3:30—"He [Jesus] must increase, but I must decrease."

[86]John 15:5, 8—"I am the vine, ye are the branches: He that abideth in me, and I in him, the same bringeth forth much fruit: for without me ye can do nothing. . . . Herein is my Father glorified, that ye bear much fruit; so shall ye be my disciples."

[87]Romans 8:13—"For if ye live after the flesh, ye shall die: but if ye through the Spirit do mortify the deeds of the body, ye shall live."

In Galatians 2:20, Paul most clearly stated the truth that our "life" comes by dying to ourselves: "I am crucified with Christ: nevertheless I live; yet not I, but Christ liveth in me: and the life which I now live in the flesh I live by the faith of the Son of God, who loved me, and gave himself for me."

Peter speaks of the reality that God lives through us when he says that we are "partakers of the divine nature." Having received "all things that pertain unto life and godliness," believers are exhorted to be diligent in adding to their "faith virtue; and to virtue knowledge; and to knowledge temperance; and to temperance patience; and to patience godliness; and to godliness brotherly kindness; and to brotherly kindness charity." These qualities are a manifestation of the character of Christ. "For if these things be in you, and abound, they make you that ye shall neither be barren nor unfruitful in the knowledge of our Lord Jesus Christ."[88]

As we seek God in order to renew our minds, we gain a deeper level of understanding of the fact that, as believers in Christ, we no longer have lives of our own. We have been purchased by the blood of Jesus and are His servants.[89] The type and amount of fruit in our lives will depend upon how completely we abide in Him. One of the most startling statements Jesus made with respect to what He wants to do through us is recorded in John 14:12: "Verily, verily, I say unto you, He that believeth on me, the works that I do shall he do also; and greater works than these shall he do; because I go unto my Father."

Have confidence that if the study of law is one of the "works" that Jesus wants to do through you, He will enable you to do it.[90] If the study and practice of law are part of the "good works" that God has ordained that you do,[91] know that His grace is sufficient and that He will make His strength perfect in your weakness.[92]

With these truths as the basis for confidence in your calling to study law, let us look at some practical ways to put on the character of Christ as you study.

---

[88]*See* II Peter 1:3–8.

[89]I Corinthians 7:22–23—"For he that is called in the Lord, being a servant, is the Lord's freeman: likewise also he that is called, being free, is Christ's servant. Ye are bought with a price; be not ye the servants of men."

[90]I Thessalonians 5:24—"Faithful is he that calleth you, who also will do it."

[91]Ephesians 2:10—"For we are his workmanship created in Christ Jesus unto good works, which God hath before ordained that we should walk in them."

[92]II Corinthians 12:9—"And he said unto me, My grace is sufficient for thee: for my strength is made perfect in weakness. Most gladly therefore will I rather glory in my infirmities, that the power of Christ may rest upon me."

Approach to Studying Law

The study of law is much different than other academic disciplines. Most students are familiar with the process of listening to lectures, reading materials, and taking tests that require them to recall information learned in the course of study.

Legal study involves more than facts and information because it requires an understanding of principles and their applications. The first challenge a student faces is comprehending the nature, implications, and exceptions to the many complicated legal principles and rules in the law school courses. At the same time, a student needs to learn to think logically, using both inductive and deductive reasoning to apply the principles in new situations, enabling him to arrive at just results.

The study of law involves a constant tension between learning the whole and the parts, just like putting together a five-hundred-piece puzzle without having the advantage of seeing the finished picture. All the pieces are there, and you know that they should all fit together some way, but it is a slow process that takes concentration and endurance. If you could understand the "big picture" of a legal subject before you began studying, it would be much easier, just as it is easier to do a puzzle if you have a completed puzzle picture in front of you. But with the law, one does not really see the whole until all of the parts are in place. Yet, the position of the parts is difficult to locate without seeing the whole picture. So, one takes it one step at a time and looks for the relationships between principles (pieces of the puzzle)—by analogy, logic, and precedent—to build the picture of the law in a particular subject area. Often, students say that a course did not "come together" until the very end when most of the pieces were present and they could see the big picture.

In addition to studying the pieces or principles in a particular course, one also has to understand the combination of the courses in a legal framework that prepares them to be competent in the practice of law. Few legal problems involve only one area of the law, and an attorney must be familiar enough with many areas to be able to ask the right questions of the client in order to get the necessary information. In addition to factual questions (such as whether the light was red or green), there are always legal questions that must be answered (such as whether one could turn right on a red light in a particular state).

Oftentimes, an attorney knows enough about the law to know that there are certain legal issues involved, but he does not necessarily know the law well enough to know immediately how to resolve those issues. That is why legal research is so important. Knowing how to find the applicable legal rules and principles, and then by logic or analogy applying those principles to your client's situation, is the essence of practicing law. So, both knowing the substantive law and researching its applications are essential to preparing for the practice of law.

Skills Preparation

In addition to learning the applicable law, an effective attorney must also communicate his conclusions to his client, develop a strategy in advocating his position, and convince others that his position is just. These functions of an attorney involve advocacy, mediation, and counseling skills. You will have the opportunity to take courses to help you develop skills in each of these areas.

Advocacy is the art of communicating both information and a perspective in a way that the listener will want to agree. It requires a complete understanding of the relevant law, a mastery of the facts, and a wise strategy to appeal to the logic and heart of the listener. Whether it is before a judge or a jury, clear communication is essential in both oral and written advocacy. A good advocate will discern the motives and mind-sets of his listeners, and use penetrating questions and pertinent stories just as Jesus did. The goal of advocacy is to persuade others to accept and act upon what the advocate says. As a Christian attorney, your role is to be an advocate for truth and for righteous causes, regardless of whether you ever appear in a courtroom.

Advocacy is not the only skill necessary to be a good lawyer. A lawyer must also be a mediator. Even if one does not become involved in a mediation or arbitration practice, an attorney needs to be able to understand both sides of the story and work to resolve or reconcile the differences. Even apart from being attorneys, we as Christians have the ministry of reconciliation given to us by Christ.[93] We must be able to explain to others God's position with respect to man's sinfulness and the means of salvation God has provided. We must be able to help others understand their own sinfulness and their need to be personally reconciled to God through Christ.

Another important aspect of the practice of law is counseling with people to help them resolve their legal problems and often, their personal problems. Many legal problems are rooted in unresolved spiritual problems as well. Legal counseling requires an understanding of human nature and also of the different motivational gifts that people have. It requires patience, sensitivity, and discernment. Wisdom must be demonstrated in deciding what questions should be asked and

[93]II Corinthians 5:18—"And all things are of God, who hath reconciled us to himself by Jesus Christ, and hath given to us the ministry of reconciliation."

how they should be asked. Creativity and discretion must be used in choosing a strategy and in interacting with opposing parties. It should be obvious that reliance upon the Holy Spirit's direction is essential when a lawyer is involved in his counseling role.

All of these functions and skills give you a glimpse of what it will be like as an attorney and why the proper approach to the study of law is so important. If one is motivated by pride or selfish ambition to be a lawyer, the dedication and thoroughness necessary to be a conscientious student may be lacking. If a student has the wrong motives for studying law, the student will not see the importance of going through the long process of putting the pieces together. Such a student will try to "cut corners" just to get by, thinking that the only goal is to pass the law school exams and the Bar exam in order to become a lawyer. Such a student will not be applauded in the Oak Brook College of Law, regardless of his grade point average.

The legal profession is an honored profession built upon service and integrity. To the degree that such an image of the profession has been tarnished, Oak Brook College students should want to restore it. This will be done only by humble reliance upon God, prayer, and diligent effort to learn the "pieces" of the legal puzzle.

Law students should think long-term and constantly ask the question, How would I resolve this question using Biblical principles? This mind-set challenges a student to study actively and to analyze whether the current status of the law is as one thinks it should be. The question should be asked, Why or why not? By always keeping in mind the goal of being a servant dedicated to helping people, one can resist the temptation to "just get by."

Also, if a law student constantly asks the Lord, *What do you want me to learn here so that I am prepared for what You have for me in the future*? the student will maintain a strong sense of purpose in studying law and will experience God's specific guidance on a daily basis.

Everyone is gifted with different abilities, and one's performance in law school is not the important issue. It is the effort and the attitude of the heart that count, because in the long run, when you are placed in that privileged position of representing people's personal and legal interests, their confidence in you will not be based upon your grades in law school. It will be based upon your *character*. Approach your legal studies with the character of Christ and you will become a Christian attorney, not just a humanistic-minded attorney who professes a faith in Jesus.

The Court Systems

In your first year of law school, you will read many cases in which judges decide legal issues raised by the opposing parties in the case. A civil case arises when there is a conflict, injury, or difference of opinion, and one party is seeking damages or equitable relief from a court. In other words, the parties either could not or would not work out the conflict without the oversight of a higher authority. After the parties clarify the legal and factual issues, a judge or a jury (depending upon whether the parties are entitled to a jury trial and have chosen one) considers the evidence and decides the issues of fact, and the judge resolves the questions of law.

In criminal cases, it is always a governmental entity that brings a suit against the defendant for violating a specific criminal statute. Generally, a criminal defendant is entitled to a jury trial unless the crime is punishable by fine only, such as with minor traffic offenses. In criminal cases, the victim of the criminal activity is not the plaintiff but will likely be a witness. The victim may or may not receive any restitution for crimes such as theft or burglary, depending upon the judge and the sentencing guidelines in a particular jurisdiction.

While it is true that certain types of disputes must first be heard on an administrative hearing level, the trial court level is generally where an initial complaint or petition is filed. In a complaint, the plaintiff or petitioner describes the wrong allegedly committed by the defendant and the type of relief the plaintiff is seeking from the defendant. A plaintiff often pleads several "causes of action" against the defendant, because there is a legal doctrine that a plaintiff is limited to one opportunity to raise all the claims related to the same factual circumstances that he has against the defendant.

The defendant may also have a claim or claims against the plaintiff related to the same factual circumstances. Such claims of the defendant are called *counterclaims*. With respect to the counterclaims, the defendant actually becomes a plaintiff and the plaintiff becomes the defendant.

The party that files the complaint first is the one whose name appears first in the name of the case. For example, *Smith v. Jones* means that Smith was the original plaintiff and Jones was the original defendant. In a criminal case, such as the *State of Illinois v. Peterson,* the government entity is the plaintiff.

If either party is not satisfied with the way the trial court interpreted or applied the law in the case, that party may appeal the issues of law to an appellate court. In fact, both parties could appeal, but generally only the losing party does so. In most cases, an appellate court will not reexamine the issues of fact. It will consider only the evidence in the "record," which is the transcript of what was said at trial and the tangible evidence presented. Only if the ruling of the trial court is against the "manifest weight of the evidence" will an appellate court reverse a finding of fact by the trial court. Most cases are appealed because one party thinks the trial court made a mistake on one or more questions of law in the case.

When a case is appealed, sometimes the order of the names changes. For example, if Jones in the previous case lost and was appealing, the name of the case at the appellate level might change to *Jones v. Smith*. Even if the procedural rules require a change in the order of the names, it is still the same case.

After a case is decided at the trial level and one party appeals the case, the court that hears the appeal is called an intermediate-level appellate court. It is intermediate because there is also a supreme court or court of highest appeal. If one of the parties thinks that the appellate court made a wrong ruling, he can petition to have the case heard by the court of highest review. In most cases, the court of highest review has the discretion to hear or not hear the case. Some cases, however, because of their importance (such as a death penalty case), are always heard by the supreme court, if requested. In fact, in some cases, the procedural rules provide that an appellant—the one appealing the trial court decision—can appeal directly to the supreme court and bypass the intermediate-level appellate court.

The United States judicial system is different from many other countries' judicial systems because of the concept of federalism. The national or federal government was formed after the state or colonial governments had existed for many years. The federal jurisdiction consists only of the authority specifically delegated to the federal government by the terms of the Constitution. Only Congress has authority to enact laws with respect to certain types of issues and subject matter. The remaining authority was retained by the states or by the people. Limitations of the federal jurisdiction apply to the judicial system as well as to the legislative and executive branches. So, in the United States, we have both state courts and federal courts.

Federal courts can hear only those disputes or issues that involve federal questions based upon federal law and certain disputes in which one party is a citizen of one state and the other party is a citizen of another state. All other issues and disputes are heard in state courts. For example, marital matters are not within the jurisdiction of the federal courts and are heard only in state courts. But bankruptcy cases are heard only in federal courts, because bankruptcy is an area of law exclusively within the federal jurisdiction, pursuant to Article I, Section 8 of the Constitution.

When it comes to constitutional issues, state courts must hear issues involving their own constitution and generally, federal courts will hear issues involving the federal constitution. As you might expect, oftentimes cases involve both state and federal issues, or state and federal constitutional questions; in such cases, a party can bring his case to either court.

Whether it is the state court or federal court system, a three-tier system of courts exists: the trial court, the intermediate appellate court, and the court of highest appeal. In state court, the trial court is usually called a *circuit, district*, or *superior* court. In federal court, it is called the district court. At the intermediate level, the court is usually called a district court of appeals on the state level and a circuit court of appeals on the federal level. Of course, the highest court of appeal on the federal level and in most state court systems is the supreme court, but in some state court systems the court of highest appeal is called the court of appeals.

It is important to remember that we have a dual system of courts in the United States. One is within the national or federal jurisdiction; the other is within each state. It is a serious misconception to think that every case can be appealed to the Supreme Court of the United States. Such an assumption reveals a lack of understanding of the important principles of federalism and the two systems of courts we have in this country.

It is of interest to note that while the term *federal* is commonly understood to mean the national government, that is not the true meaning of the word. *Federal* is derived from the Latin word *foedus*, which means covenant or compact. Properly understood, a federal government is a description of the relationship among civil governments rather than a particular body of government. Over time, the adjective *federal* has been converted to a noun meaning a particular government, much like the adjective *catholic* has been converted to mean a particular denomination. *Federal* is the appropriate term to describe the constitutional diffusion or division of authority between the government of general jurisdiction (state) and the government of limited jurisdiction (national). Thus, federalism is the legal and political doctrine that requires the recognition of, and the respect for, the jurisdictional authority of each government, state and federal. While the jurisdictions are separate, they are joined together by the United States Constitution.

The federal model has Biblical precedent. The nation of Israel was federal in nature because there were twelve distinct tribes or political units, joined together by a national covenant with God. God, through Moses, told the people that if they would keep His covenant, they would be unto Him a "kingdom of priests, and a holy nation."[94] Then Moses called the elders together and asked for their decision on whether they would enter into this covenant with God. The people answered by saying that they would do all that the Lord had spoken.[95] Each tribe had its own elders and local rulers, but the nation was joined together by a national covenant with God and each other.

The foregoing description of the judicial systems will help you understand the context of the cases you will read in your first year of legal study. Most of the assigned cases will be opinions written by an intermediate appellate court or by a supreme court. In the state courts, rarely is there an opinion written by the trial court, and in the federal court, the district court often does not publish its opinions.

Now that you know that there is a difference between state and federal cases and that court opinions are written by judges at different levels, we want to discuss how you can identify and find those cases and other important sources of legal information.

Legal Research Tools

Reading cases is an important exercise in learning how to apply legal principles to reach a conclusion to resolve a dispute. But what if you need to find out what legal principles apply to the situation? In such situations, skills in legal research are essential.

When researching a legal issue, the first place to look is always the applicable statutes. If the issue is a matter of state law, you would look in the state statutes. If it involves federal law, you would look to the United States Code. If there is an applicable statute, it may directly answer your question, but more likely it will not, and you will have to read cases to learn how the courts have interpreted and applied the particular statute involved.

Statutes are the specific laws enacted by the legislative body of a jurisdiction. The statutes are generally printed in two forms. One set is a publication of the laws only; another set, called annotated statutes, contains the statutes plus a brief synopsis of cases interpreting

---

[94]Exodus 19:6—"And ye shall be unto me a kingdom of priests, and an holy nation. These are the words which thou shalt speak unto the children of Israel."

[95]Exodus 19:7–8—"And Moses came and called for the elders of the people, and laid before their faces all these words which the Lord commanded him. And all the people answered together, and said, All that the Lord hath spoken we will do. And Moses returned the words of the people unto the Lord."

and applying the statutes. For example, Illinois has a nine-volume set of statutes titled *Illinois Compiled Statutes*, and there is another set of books called *Illinois Compiled Statutes Annotated*. The compiled statute volumes are the "official publication," and any references to the statutes should be cited to this publication. The annotated statutes contain the same information but are published by private companies and therefore are not the official publication.

The annotated statutes are very useful in locating cases, law review articles, and other related sources that interpret, discuss, or apply the statutes. Annotated statutes also contain references to additional related information in other research books such as legal digests, legal encyclopedias, and legal formbooks.

After you read the statute or statutes and the annotations, you will then read the "on point" cases in the "reporters." Case reporters are sets of books containing the published opinions of the courts. As with statutes, there are federal reporters and state reporters. There are also official reporters and unofficial reporters for cases in each jurisdiction. The reporters are published in volumes numbered consecutively, and most of the reporters are now publishing cases in a second or third set. For example, if a case is located at 12 F.2d 135, it means that the case is located in volume 12 of the second set of the Federal Reporter on page 135.

The reporters have different names, depending upon which level of court wrote the opinions published in the set. For example, the Federal Supplement contains federal district (trial) court opinions; the Federal Reporter contains federal court of appeals decisions; the United States Reports contains the opinions of the Supreme Court of the United States. In your legal research and writing course, you will learn more about the reporter system, including regional reporters and state reporters.

After you locate the relevant cases that give you guidance in answering a legal question, you will want to make sure that the rulings or decisions in those opinions have not been reversed or overruled. For example, you may have a decision by an intermediate-level appellate court that ruled on a legal issue, but the case was appealed to a supreme court and the supreme court reversed the appellate court decision. If you had read only the appellate court opinion and did not check to see if there was a subsequent opinion on that same case, you would be making a serious error that could even be considered malpractice. Even the subsequent history of Supreme Court opinions needs to be checked, because the high court has been known to reverse itself and overrule a previous decision.

Research tools that you use to check the subsequent history of a case are called the *Shepard's* citators. With one of the *Shepard's* citators, a case citator, you can find out not only whether a particular case has been reversed, overruled, or vacated, but it can also be used to locate other cases that have cited the particular case you are "shepardizing." So in addition to the annotated statutes, the applicable *Shepard's* case citator is a useful tool to locate other cases relevant to the legal issue you are researching. *Shepard's* also publishes citators to discover the subsequent history of a statute, which would be very important if you are not sure that you have the latest version of a statute.

If the legal issue you are researching does not involve a statute, you have a different arsenal of legal research tools that you can use. If you did not know much about a particular area of law, you could look up the topic in a legal encyclopedia such as *Corpus Juris Secundum* or *American Jurisprudence*. These sets of books discuss most areas of law in a general way and cite cases and other resources in support of the discussion. Law Review articles are also a good resource to obtain background information on current legal issues in the area. This initial research will help you locate a Key Number or commonly used *Words and Phrases* regarding the area of law.

Key Numbers are research tools developed by the West Publishing Company (now known as West Group) to locate cases and other information pertinent to specific legal topics. Once you locate the one or two most "on point" Key Numbers, you can locate cases, references to encyclopedia sections, and even relevant legal forms for pleadings or document drafting relevant to the issue. The West Key Number System and the research schemes developed by other legal book publishers are fast-track ways to find the information you need to answer legal questions.

Other very important research tools are legal digests. A digest is a set of books containing short descriptions of cases pertinent to legal topics. The topics are arranged alphabetically and are tied into West's Key Numbering System. By looking at a topic in the digest's subject index or by using the words and phrases index or the table of cases, you can find other cases that address the specific issues you are researching.

Lastly, you should know about headnotes. Headnotes are sentence summaries of what a court has said about legal concepts or topics discussed in a case. Headnotes are printed before the court opinion and are very helpful in determining the issues resolved by the court. The headnotes also direct you to the exact location within the opinion where the court discussed a particular topic. Headnotes are written by the publishers of the case reporters and are not part of the official opinion. For that reason, a student should not rely on the accuracy of the headnotes and should read the case before making any decision about the relevancy of a case to the issue of law being researched. Headnotes are very helpful in the initial research stage because each headnote includes a Key Number, which makes it easy to determine if the case contains any discussion of an issue you are researching.

Approach to Reading and Briefing Cases

During the study of law, you will read many cases. Reading cases is not done for the purpose of gathering information, as is the situation with most academic reading. In your substantive courses, you will read cases to discover and understand legal principles, to gain skill in identifying factual and legal issues, and to learn how to logically analyze the issues to reach a correct legal conclusion. Attaining these skills is certainly a major part of the legal educational process and is exactly what you will be expected to do on an examination. Therefore, it is a serious mistake not to read and brief the cases assigned in each course.

Reading and briefing cases is a skill developed over time and through experience. Later in law school, reading cases should become fairly easy, and briefing them can probably be done in an abbreviated format, but not when you first begin. Extra time will be needed to read a case because the substance of what you are reading will be so unfamiliar and the terminology so foreign. A legal dictionary will be a much-used tool during the first year of legal study as you read words involving procedure and substantive law with which you are not yet familiar.

In the study of law, there are often processes or procedures used to develop necessary legal skills. Briefing cases is one of those procedures to gain an essential skill. A brief of a case is a written exercise by which one summarizes, analyzes, and critiques the written opinion of a court's decision. The brief is also used to record, for future reference, how legal principles were applied in a particular factual concept. This helps one remember and understand the principles being learned. Briefs can then be referred to and used to create outlines of principles and law that must be understood for exams and for legal practice.

The process of briefing cases develops analytical and writing skills, and the brief itself helps one understand some of the "puzzle pieces" of the course. The brief written for a case is not nearly as important as the learning process that takes place as you analyze the case to construct a brief. The skills learned by briefing cases prepare you to properly answer examination questions and to be more efficient and effective in legal research and writing, an attorney's prominent responsibility.

Let us look more closely at a brief's purpose, content, and suggested format. Case briefing involves at least seven steps. While some may divide a brief into more parts than those discussed here, the goal in briefing is the same. Each step in the analytical process is necessary to develop reasoning skills and to understand the court's rationale for its decision.

The first step to analyzing any case is to read it! Read the case to obtain a working knowledge of the story it tells. Find out why the parties are in court and what the court is being asked to decide.

The next step is to identify the "Nature of the Case" and the procedural matters that the court is addressing. This includes general background information about how the case reached this court and the type of claims being made by the plaintiff. This information is important because it gives you the context of the case and is helpful in understanding the authority that the court has to render a binding decision.

Third, a student needs to summarize the story or the facts. The facts tell what happened to give rise to the controversy. In some cases, "what happened" is the key question that needs to be answered. Such cases are said to involve "questions of fact." In other cases, the facts are clear and the only question involves the correct application of the law to the facts. These cases involve "questions of law." In your brief, you should write down only the important facts—the facts that are relevant to the outcome of the case.

Next, a student should identify the legal questions or issues the court is being asked to decide. It is always good to write your issue statement in the form of a *whether* question, including some pertinent facts. An example is "whether the defendant was negligent because he failed to mop the floor after a spill of milk." Oftentimes, a case involves more than one issue.

In such situations, the court must decide the preliminary issues before it can decide the main issue. If the court must decide more than one issue to resolve the case, each issue should be included in your brief. However, only include issues that are related to the subject matter you are studying. For example, you would not want to include procedural issues when the purpose of the case is to teach you something about what constitutes an "offer" in contract law.

Fifth, you should ask yourself the following question: What law or principle did the court use to resolve each issue in the case? The answer to this question will give you the rule that the court applied. The *rule* must be distinguished from the *ruling* of the court. The *rule* is the foundational legal principle that the court applied to the facts to reach its conclusion. The *ruling* is the holding of the court or its conclusion.

Oftentimes a case is assigned to show how a court expanded or extended an existing principle to resolve a particular dispute. The court may decide the case by making an analogy between the principles used in previous related cases, or the court may derive a "new" principle based upon precedent. The point is that the *rule* step in writing a brief involves discerning the laws or principles upon which the court based its decision.

The sixth step to analyzing a case could be called the *application* section. This part of the brief discusses how the facts and the law fit together. You would describe how the court integrated the facts into a discussion of the law to reach its conclusion on the issues. This could also be called the *analysis* section of the brief, because it includes the basic logic of the court's decision. By going through this process, you will learn more about legal reasoning and will develop your own ability to think through the steps needed to reach a correct legal conclusion. This is the same type of analysis a student needs to make when writing answers to essay examination questions.

Finally, you should conclude your analysis by identifying how and why the court answered the question(s). The conclusion is essentially answering the issue statement in either a positive or negative way; for example, "The court found that it was negligence for the defendant not to mop the floor after knowing about the spill of milk." In addition to the legal resolution of the issue, the conclusion should include a brief explanation of the court's rationale or reasoning for its conclusion. This statement could be something such as, "because the defendant could have reasonably foreseen that someone would slip and fall on the milk." The conclusion is the ruling or holding of the case. It will be used by other courts as precedent to decide similar cases in the future.

If it seems as though some parts of the brief overlap, they do. However, each part has a distinct purpose and is necessary to proceed to the next step in the analysis. Briefing cases in this way is necessary to develop logical thinking skills and the ability to distinguish relevant and important facts from unnecessary information.

The following is an edited court opinion and a sample brief with commentary on each section.

Jones v. City of Prairie City
Court of Appeals, 1987
86 Or. App. 701, 740 P.2d 236

Van Hoomissen, Judge.

This is an action to recover damages for negligence. Defendant's motion to dismiss was allowed. ORCP 21 A (8). Plaintiff appeals. The issue is whether the plaintiff's complaint states a claim. We conclude that it does and reverse.

Plaintiff, a minor child, was bitten by a dog running at large in Prairie City (City). City's police department impounded the dog on the day that plaintiff was bitten. Two days later, City destroyed the dog. It had not been tested for rabies before it was destroyed and, because it could not thereafter be determined whether or not it was rabid, plaintiff had to undergo a series of rabies inoculations.

Plaintiff sued City, alleging that it was negligent in destroying the dog without waiting 10 days, in violation of Or. Rev. Stat. 609.090. City moved to dismiss the complaint for failure to state a claim for relief. The trial court held that plaintiff is not a member of the class of persons intended to be protected by Or. Rev. Stat. 609.090 and granted City's motion.

Or. Rev. Stat. 609.090 provides, in relevant part:

"(1) When any dog is found running at large in any county, precinct or city . . . or when a dog is a public nuisance . . . , every chief of police, constable, sheriff, or deputy of either, or other police or dog control officer shall impound it. . . . .

(2) . . . If no owner appears to redeem a dog within the allotted time, or if the dog has been impounded as a public nuisance for killing or injuring a person, it shall be killed in a humane manner. . . .

(3) Notwithstanding the provisions of subsection (2) of this section, any dog impounded for biting a person shall be held for not less than 10 days before redemption or destruction to determine if the dog is rabid."

Plaintiff argues that the statute is narrowly and clearly written, that there could be no intended beneficiary other than the person bitten by the dog and that there could be no harm to be prevented other than that which plaintiff sustained. City argues that the only purpose of the statute is to give public bodies authority to destroy dangerous dogs, that the 10-day requirement was enacted at the request of the Oregon Health Department and that the legislative history suggests that its only purpose was to permit the destruction of dangerous dogs and not to create a basis for a private claim for dog bite victims.

The issues in a negligence case are "whether defendant's conduct caused a forseeable kind of harm to an interest protected against that kind of negligent invasion, and whether the conduct creating the risk of that kind of harm was unreasonable under the circumstances." *Donaca v. Curry County*, 303 Or. 30, 38, 734 P.2d 1339 (1987). There are various methods of establishing what is forseeable and what is reasonable. A plaintiff may rely on common law standards of care or on a statute which itself establishes a standard. *Shahtout v. Emco Garbage* Co., 298 Or. 598, 695 P.2d 897 (1985).

Further, "[w]hen a plaintiff (or a defendant seeking to prove negligence on a plaintiff's part) invokes a governmental rule in support of that theory, the question is whether the rule, though not itself intended to create a civil claim, nevertheless so fixes the legal standard of conduct that there is no question of due care left for the fact finder to determine; in other words, that noncompliance with the rule is negligence as a matter of law." 298 Or. at 601, 695 P.2d 897.

Unless a court can justifiably say that no reasonable fact finder could find the risk forseeable or that the defendant's conduct fell below acceptable standards, the questions of foreseeability and reasonableness are for the fact finder to decide. *Fazzolari v. Portland School Dist.* No. 1J, 303 Or. 1, 17, 734 P.2d 1326 (1987); *Donaca v. Curry Co. supra*, 303 Or. at 38, 734 P.2d 1339.

In this case, it is at least arguably forseeable that, if a dog is destroyed before the time needed for testing for rabies expires, a person bitten by the dog would have to undergo treatment against rabies. The statute provides that City could have impounded the dog for the necessary

10 days, thus preventing it from running at large. In the absence of some explanation for a need to destroy dog in less than 10 days, a reasonable fact finder could conclude that City's conduct was unreasonable. The fact that the legislative history of Or. Rev. Stat. 609.090 does not indicate an intent to create a new cause of action does not prevent the statute from being used to measure the standard of care of officials who impound dogs under the authority of that statute in determining whether City's conduct was reasonable under the circumstances. *Shahtout v. Emco Garbage Co., supra.*

Reversed and remanded.

Jones v. City of Prairie

Oregon Court of Appeals (1987)

Nature of Case

Plaintiff (P) filed a negligence action against City (D), which was dismissed upon D's motion. P appealed the trial court's granting of the motion to dismiss to the Court of Appeals of Oregon.

Notice that this information does not tell the story of the case. It deals primarily with the history of the case.

Facts

P, a minor child, was bitten by a dog running at large in City. City police impounded the dog, but destroyed the dog two days later, before the dog was tested for rabies. A statute required impounded dogs to be held for ten days. P sued, claiming that the City was negligent by prematurely destroying the dog, thereby preventing rabies testing and requiring P to undergo precautionary treatments for rabies. The trial court dismissed the case on City's motion to dismiss for failure to state a claim.

These statements tell the story by summarizing the important facts. You have a basic understanding of what happened.

Issue

Whether the City could be subject to a negligence claim for destroying the impounded dog within two days, rather than waiting the ten days required by statute.

This is the question or issue the court must answer.

Rule

Where D breaches a statutory duty, resulting in damage to the plaintiff, D can be held negligent if such harm is a reasonably foreseeable result of the breach of duty.

This states the legal principle that guided the court in its decision. The court was applying the principle of negligence law, which states that if a duty is breached, and if the breach caused a reasonably foreseeable injury, defendant can be responsible for damages.

Application

The court held that the statute governing the destruction of impounded dogs creates a statutory duty that should have been adhered to by the City. Destruction of the dog prior to the expiration of the statutory period is evidence of a breach of that duty. However, there can be no negligence unless that breach of duty results in a foreseeable injury to the plaintiff. Because the stated purpose of the statute is to determine whether the dog is rabid, the court held that a trier of fact could find that the City's action was unreasonable and that P's injury was forseeable.

This section applies the rule to the facts. Each element of a negligence cause of action was discussed to determine if Plaintiff had a sufficient claim. The duty was discussed in the first sentence; breach of that duty was discussed in the second; and causation and damages were discussed in the remainder of the section.

Conclusion

The court reversed the trial court's decision granting the motion to dismiss, finding that City could be found negligent by breaching its statutory duty owed to P, resulting in foreseeable injury to P. P is entitled to a trial to determine if the damage P suffered was a reasonably forseeable consequence of not holding the dog for ten days.

This section gives the final conclusion of the court. It includes an answer to the question asked of the court.

Approach to Other Readings

Cases are not the only thing you will read in your legal studies. Hornbooks and commercial outlines (e.g., *Gilbert Law Summaries*) are also used to put the pieces together. As was initially stated, cases are read and analyzed to develop certain skills, not necessarily for the purpose of learning "black letter law." In fact, you may be assigned a case to read that articulates a minority opinion on a particular legal issue. Therefore, it is a mistake to assume that just because a particular case says the law is a certain way, the position of that court is consistent with the majority or generally accepted legal principles. For these reasons, you will need to read and study other sources of legal information. You need some type of outline of the substantive law in each course and a resource to fill in the details and help put everything in perspective.

The commercial outlines generally used by OBCL students are *Gilbert Law Summaries*. These outlines can be thought of as the skeleton of the course. They are useful to help one see the connection between one concept of the law and another. These outlines give students the big picture and help them see where the cases fit in and what is to be studied later on in the course. But a skeleton cannot stand alone. It needs muscle and flesh. That is where hornbooks come in.

A hornbook is a one-volume treatise on a subject; it discusses in more detail the legal principles and the reasons for those principles that you study. It also contains information on the historical development and the current trends in the law. Therefore, not everything you read in a hornbook is "black letter law," but it does give an additional explanation as well as the context of the law you are studying.

Some students think that it takes too much time to read the hornbook, and they do not consider it very useful in preparing to take an exam. This is a mistake! Your purpose in law school is not just to take exams. In fact, some students may do well on exams but be complete failures as lawyers because they have never learned to read through larger quantities of material and discern what is relevant and important and what is not. By reading the hornbook assignments, you will have a deeper understanding of the important concepts and a richer appreciation for the context of the law. In the process, you will also develop the skill of distinguishing the good and interesting information from the truly important information.

A student might be able to "get by" by studying only the commercial outlines, without reading much in the hornbooks. You may even do well on the exams because you know the main points of law. But if you neglect reading the hornbooks, you will be inhibiting the development of certain skills that will be very important after you graduate. Distinguishing the relevant from the irrelevant and the important from the interesting are essential skills to learn as you undertake the awesome responsibility of an officer of the court and a trusted legal counselor, mediator, and advocate. Remember, your goal is to "study to show thyself approved unto God." If you do this, God will be able to use you after you graduate in ways you could never imagine.

Approach to Daily Study

As you begin your legal studies, you must take the attitude that you are preparing for the Olympics. You are studying not just for midterms, finals, or even the First-Year Law Students' Exam; you are studying for the California Bar exam and the professional practice of law. Olympic athletes train for years for an event that may last only minutes. Consistent and concentrated effort is necessary. The seeds of time you sow today will reap lasting benefits tomorrow and in the future. If you are called, God's grace is more than sufficient. In your weakness, His strength is made perfect. Always begin your study time by committing it to the Lord. His promise is that He will establish your thoughts.[96] Because of all the other responsibilities many law students have and because of their limited time, it is certainly important that God establish your thoughts and give you discernment, alertness, understanding, wisdom, and diligence.

God tells us to think not for tomorrow.[97] He warns us against making selfish plans for the future, because we know not what a day may bring forth or whether our lives will be taken this very day.[98] While we are not to worry about tomorrow, we *are* to plan. A wise man plans before he goes to battle or before he builds a house, lest he begin and not have the resources to win the battle or to complete the project.[99] Similarly, law students need to plan their study time.

Each student should have a flexible plan and a systematic approach to the study of law. The plan should be broken down into steps, and concentrated effort should be used to accomplish each step. Some familiar sayings illustrate the point: "Plan your work, and then work your plan"; "Success by a yard is hard, but by an inch it is a

---

[96]Proverbs 16:3—"Commit thy works unto the LORD, and thy thoughts shall be established."

[97]Matthew 6:34—"Take therefore no thought for the morrow: for the morrow shall take thought for the things of itself. Sufficient unto the day is the evil thereof." Proverbs 27:1—"Boast not thyself of tomorrow; for thou knowest not what a day may bring forth."

[98]Luke 12:16–21—"And he spake a parable unto them, saying, The ground of a certain rich man brought forth plentifully: And he thought within himself, saying, What shall I do, because I have no room where to bestow my fruits? And he said, This will I do: I will pull down my barns, and build greater; and there will I bestow all my fruits and my goods. And I will say to my soul, Soul, thou hast much goods laid up for many years; take thine ease, eat, drink, and be merry. But God said unto him, Thou fool, this night thy soul shall be required of thee: then whose shall those things be, which thou hast provided? So is he that layeth up treasure for himself, and is not rich toward God."

[99]Luke 14:28–31—"For which of you, intending to build a tower, sitteth not down first, and counteth the cost, whether he have sufficient to finish it? Lest haply, after he hath laid the foundation, and is not able to finish it, all that behold it begin to mock him, Saying, This man began to build, and was not able to finish. Or what king, going to make war against another king, sitteth not down first, and consulteth whether he be able with ten thousand to meet him that cometh against him with twenty thousand?"

cinch." But your plan should be flexible, giving God the liberty to direct your steps in ways better than you can plan.

Because each student's situation is different, it is very difficult to recommend a specific approach to study time. However, some general principles can be incorporated into any plan and, if implemented, will result in success. The first, most basic principle is to **plan a time to study every day**. A deadly trap is to think that you can take it easy for a while and catch up later. Oftentimes, the time you thought you would have later is not there, or the time needed to complete a particular project is longer than anticipated.

The first thing you need to include in your plan every day is your time with Jesus. As you read His Word, your soul and spirit are fed. As you pray, you are given direction and peace, knowing that your Heavenly Father will sustain you. There is no more important time of the day than the time you spend with the Lord. At all costs, do not neglect reading, memorizing, and meditating on His Word. The promises of success for these disciplines are clear, and the success will be according to His standards, not man's.

One student at another law school did not neglect his time with God while in law school; he also purposed not to neglect his family. Although he was not one of the top students in his class, after graduation, God opened the door for him to be the clerk to a federal district court judge for several years. He was so well respected by the judge that the judge gave him major responsibilities, including overseeing all the complex civil litigation, conducting seminars on dispute resolution, and drafting many court opinions. After leaving that position, this graduate became the lead counsel for a prominent Christian litigation group and continues to have a significant influence for the kingdom of God. Be faithful to God so that you will experience more completely His presence in your life and will receive clear direction for ministry.

Whether you are married or single, you cannot put your family on the shelf for four and a half years. Within the family jurisdiction, you will need to spend time with those God has given you as a family. The specific times will change as circumstances arise and different seasons occur, but you should keep your family as your highest priority next to God. Your family is your greatest support. You need them, but they also need you. Emotional absence from the ones closest to you will be very destructive to your legal studies. But emotional closeness with your family will enable you to do more in less time, and you will have an understanding support group who will help to sustain you in the difficult and intense times.

With these two priorities scheduled in your mind as the most important (even if they do not take most of your time), you then need to decide on a strategic plan for studying. This plan needs to include an allocation of time and a specific approach to studying the assigned courses.

Allocation of Time

The Oak Brook College curriculum anticipates that a student will study at least 45 hours for every hour of credit earned. In the first year, a student takes courses with the total credit-hour value of 20. This means that you can anticipate spending about 900 hours in the study of law your first year. The California Bar requires a minimum of 864 hours. If you divide 900 hours by the 49 study and exam weeks of your first year, you can expect to study a minimum of 18–20 hours per week. When you first begin, you can expect your studies to take more time, until you develop a certain comfort level and efficiency with the course material. Given the fact that the first day of the week (Sunday) is dedicated to the Lord and His people, you will average studying 3–4 hours per day. That is a significant amount of time, and you will need to plan ahead.

Generally, the recommended time of study at one sitting should not be less than 20–30 minutes and not more than 2–3 hours. With this in mind, and depending on your work schedule and family commitments, the following are some suggestions:

1. 5:00 A.M.–6:30 A.M.: Personal time and time with Jesus
6:30 A.M.–7:30 or 8:00 A.M.: Study time for one subject
8:00 P.M.–9:30 or 10:00 P.M.: Study time for two subjects
Sat. 6:30 A.M.–NOON: Study time

2. 5:00 A.M.–6:30 A.M.: Personal time and time with Jesus
4:00 P.M.–6:00 P.M.: Study time for one or two subjects
8:00 P.M.–9:30 or 10:00 P.M.: Study time for one or two subjects
Sat. 1:00 P.M.–5:00 P.M.: Study time

The important point is to have a scheduled time to study and to know which course you are going to study at what time. It is important to limit the time that you study a particular course to the time allocated. This will encourage active, diligent study to accomplish a specific amount within the allocated time, rather than taking the attitude, "I will see how much I get done."

Flexibility is critical in scheduling your study. The circumstances of one day, one week, or even one month may require that you study during times other than those you scheduled, or you may even be prevented from studying at all. This happens, but if you have scheduled study times, you have a plan to which you can return when the crisis or interruption is over. You may also need to reevaluate your schedule and determine if there is a more convenient or efficient schedule that should be adopted. This is when family members can be especially helpful by considering your needs and adjusting the family schedule to make it easier on you.

Keeping either Saturday morning or afternoon free, as well as Saturday night, is strongly recommended. This gives you the liberty of having free time for family or other demands or interests without feeling guilty for not studying. If you have scheduled "free time," it should not be used for study. Other plans should be made if you need to "catch up" rather than thinking "in the back of your mind" that you can always use the free time for study. Do not give yourself such an excuse for not being diligent and active during the times that you have scheduled for study.[100]

Specific Plan for Each Course

If you talk with other students, you will find that they use a variety of study plans. Some of these plans are purposeful and are based upon the different ways one learns best. Other plans are based upon past habit or experience. The best plan of study for you will be based upon a number of factors. One factor you may want to consider is whether you are primarily an auditory or visual learner. Auditory learners would probably prefer to listen to the audio lectures first. Visual learners probably prefer to read the material first and use the audio lectures later. You will have to decide which plan is better for you.

For some students, the specific study plan is partly determined by the time and location of study. For example, if you are spending time each day driving to work, it may be a good opportunity to listen to an audio lecture to get an overview of the lesson or to review what you have already studied. If you study early in the morning when the house is quiet, you can best use this time for a concentrated study of new material. Times when there may be more interruptions could be used for less intense study, such as reviewing lecture tapes.

The pace at which one goes through the material also varies from student to student. While you must keep the pace outlined in the syllabus, some students prefer to go faster and get the big picture as soon as possible. After having read all the material, they go back and study the material in more detail and try to put together the pieces. Other students prefer to study more intensely first and review later.

[100]Proverbs 22:29—"Seest thou a man diligent in his business? he shall stand before kings; he shall not stand before mean men."

Again, the method you choose may depend on the amount of time you have at different stages in the semester.

One way students get the big picture first is by reading the *Gilbert Law Summaries* outline for a course before studying the cases and the hornbook. This is a good approach, because it is quick and can be reviewed often as you do the more in-depth study. After reading the *Gilbert's*, the cases should be read, followed by reading the hornbook to gain a more complete understanding.

With respect to reading cases, one approach that has proved to be highly successful is to read as much of the case as is necessary to understand the facts and the relevant issues and then stop to think about how you would decide the case. Having thought about the issues, you will read the remainder of the case with much more interest in order to discover how the court resolved the issues. You can then compare the court's ruling with your thoughts. This is an active form of studying because you are interacting with the material instead of simply reading it. Also, this approach will speed the development of your analytical skills and greatly enhance your ability to write accurate and complete case briefs.

The hornbook reading is more necessary when studying certain topics than it is with others. After you have read the commercial course outline and the cases, you may think that you have a solid understanding of the material. If this is true, you should skim the hornbook readings to confirm and reinforce your understanding. With other courses, the commercial course outline and the cases are just not enough. This is when you should take the time to thoroughly read the hornbook in order to grasp the substance of the legal concepts or rules. If, after reading the hornbook, you are still confused, you should seek assistance from others, including OBCL staff. If you are confused and do not get your questions answered by someone in the College office, you should feel free to contact the professor at the times and in the manner he or she has indicated.

If you follow this plan and supplement your study with the lecture tapes, you should be able to comprehend the material in each course. There are many different types of study aids being marketed today, especially to intimidated, first-year law students. Do not fall prey to this trap. Some additional commercial study aids—such as flash cards—may be beneficial as you study for finals, but do not go out and buy expensive books, tapes, or programs because you are fearful at the beginning of your legal studies. Remember, if you commit your works to God, He will establish your thoughts. The Holy Spirit leading and directing you is far better than any study aids ever could be.

The Dynamics of Learning

Throughout your legal studies, it is important to keep in mind the goals of each aspect of study. Whether you are reading and briefing cases or outlining portions of the discussion in a hornbook, you are involved in the dynamics of learning. If you understand why you are doing something, you will have more motivation to do it well. For this reason, it is beneficial to discuss the dynamics of learning and the functions of each aspect of the study of law.

The dynamics of learning include the following:

1. Desire or interest to learn
2. Exposure to information and concepts
3. Assimilation of information and concepts
4. Distillation of information and concepts
5. Application of information and concepts

Since each of you has committed yourself to the study of law, it is safe to assume that you have a desire to learn. At least you have a desire to be an attorney and therefore, you have an interest in what must be learned to reach that goal. Different students enjoy different subjects for different reasons, but the study of all the material is necessary to reach your goal of becoming a minister of reconciliation and justice. As the Apostle Paul said, "I press toward the mark for the prize of the high calling of God in Christ Jesus (Philippians 3:14). The desire to learn should not be rooted in a motive of selfish gain but rather in a desire to be equipped to serve as the Lord directs.

Some of you have had more exposure than others to the law and to the functions of an attorney. As you begin your studies, you will probably feel overwhelmed with the amount of material to study. This is normal and should not alarm you. It is like traveling in an unfamiliar city. You do not know the street names, the landmarks, or the best routes to get to a destination. Even a map helps you only to a limited degree. Time and experience are needed to become comfortable and familiar with the surroundings. The same is true with the study of law. The new terminology, principles, and procedures must be "traveled" before you can feel competent. The outlines or maps only expose you to the material. You must work with it and digest it, which is the next dynamic.

Reading and briefing the cases, studying the hornbook, and preparing your own course outlines are all involved in the process of assimilation. Assimilating the material means that it becomes a part of you and your thinking. This takes time, practice, and repetition. With each case you read, if you do it actively as suggested, you will gain skill in assimilating legal concepts more quickly. Briefing cases forces you to work with the material and analyze exactly what the court said and did. Outlining is when you take what you learned and organize it in a way that is most meaningful to you. The goal is not making good briefs or outlines; the goal is assimilation of the material.

Outlining your courses also requires you to distill the material, just as water is reduced into a smaller opening as it goes through a funnel. All the material must be poured into your brain and processed in order to be assimilated. But as you assimilate the legal concepts, you will see relationships and similarities between the concepts, enabling you to digest the material down to the essential points. Again, the outline is not the main goal; it is the process of distillation that is essential to your legal education. That is why reading another student's outline, or even a commercial outline, has limited value. While you may obtain information from reading it, the dynamic of distillation is omitted if you do not make your own outlines.

Another very useful way to distill the information is by developing flowcharts. In fact, some students spend their time developing flowcharts rather than outlines. This certainly is permissible, because the process of distilling the material can be done by either method. For visual learners, it is very helpful to see a diagram of a course, or a particular legal concept within a course, in one "picture." As with the outlines, the flowcharts are not the main goal. The flowcharts will be most helpful to the student who developed them, because that person knows all that went into them and has progressed in the development of the skills necessary to create the flowchart successfully.

For the sake of illustration, the following sample is a partial outline of the concept of "offer" in the law of contracts, followed by a flowchart of the same concept.

I. Offer Under Common Law

A. ***Common Law offer defined:*** *At Common Law, a valid offer requires (i) a manifestation of present intent to enter into a bargain (ii) which is made in sufficiently definite terms and (iii) is communicated to the offeree. (The UCC requirement is less strict.)*

B. ***Elements of a Common Law offer***

1. Manifestation of a present intent to enter into a bargain—*contractual intent*

(a) **Preliminary negotiations:** Remember that preliminary negotiations indicate an intent to deal rather than an intent to be bound.

(1) **Auctions:** One particular issue that arises from time to time is whether bids at an auction are offers to buy, or the acceptance of the auctioneer's offer. This question becomes relevant when the seller considers the bid to be too low. If the auction was an offer, the bid would constitute acceptance and the seller is bound to the bargain. To solve this, auctions fall into one of the following categories:

(a) **Advertised *without reserve*:** If an auction is advertised as *without reserve*, an item can be withdrawn only if no bid is given within a reasonable time.

(b) **Advertised *with reserve*:** In an auction advertised as *with reserve*, an item can be withdrawn any time during the bidding (normal auctions).

(b) **Objective versus subjective standard:** Contractual intent is judged by an objective standard rather than a subjective standard. Thus, if the offeror really did not want to sell his motorcycle but communicated words sufficient to constitute an offer and which would have the effect of reasonably causing the offeree to believe that an offer was made, an offer is established.

(c) **Illusory promises are not offers:** Remember that an offer is a gift of sorts, which the offeror gives to the offeree. That gift is the power of acceptance. If the offeror can back out of the deal for any reason he wants to, an illusory promise has occurred and no offer is established. Thus, if A says to B, "I'll sell it to you if I want to," there is no offer.

2. Sufficiently definite terms—"QTIPS"

(a) **Q**uantity
(b) **T**ime
(c) **I**dentity of the parties
(d) **P**rice
(e) **S**ubject matter

Modern law will consider a contract to be sufficiently definite even when some of the terms are missing, as long as a "reasonable" term can be presumed (time for performance not mentioned—reasonable time presumed).

3. Communicated to the offeree

(a) An offer must be clearly communicated to the offeree to be binding in the contract. An offer is effective upon receipt by the offeree. The two most frequent ways that this issue comes up are instances involving rewards and advertisements.

(1) **Rewards:** One cannot claim that a reward is an offer unless he was aware of the reward at the time he performed the service.

(2) **Advertisements:** Because they are usually communicated to the public, advertisements are generally not considered offers. A narrow exception to this rule exists in advertisements that contain specific terms which would lead a reasonable person to believe that they were offers (e.g., "First ten customers will receive an additional 30% off.").

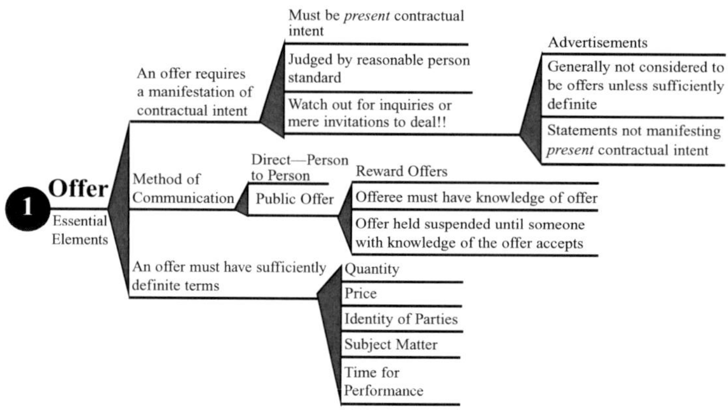

The final stage in the dynamics of learning is the application phase. This, of course, is the examination process and eventually the actual practice of law. Law exams are designed to test your ability to apply the course matter. Such a goal presupposes knowledge of the subject matter and an ability to discern the relevant issues. This is why all of the previous dynamics learned through briefing cases and outlining are so important. You cannot do the application phase if you have neglected the previous four dynamics of learning.

Whether the examination consists of multiple-choice questions or essay questions, the student will be required to go through the very same mental process used in briefing and outlining. The facts must be understood and interpreted within the framework of the legal concepts you learned. Knowing definitions and the "black letter law" is only the first step. You must then decide what the legal issues are within the factual setting and then apply the law to the facts to reach a conclusion. The ability to do this comes only from practice, practice, and more practice! Do not listen to those who tell you that briefing cases and outlining or developing flowcharts is not important. Remember, it is your responsibility to do what is necessary to prepare yourself for God's service.

If you keep these dynamics of learning in mind, you will see the relevance of what may sometimes appear to be an unnecessary exercise. What you sow, you will also reap. You will be as diligent and thorough as an attorney as you are as a student.

In all law schools, the only opportunity a student has to demonstrate his analytical skills and knowledge of substantive law is the examinations. They are like time trials: if you make it, you go on, if not, you stay back. You cannot expect to show up on the day of the time trials and run a good race if you have not practiced before. Even if you "crammed" for a few weeks before, your performance will be less than what it could—and should—have been. In the same way, do not expect to do well on exams if you have not been diligent in your studies throughout the semester. Sure, you may pass the course by cramming, but are you prepared for the practice of law?

If you can adapt the attitude of the bricklayer who said he was "building a cathedral" rather than just laying bricks, you will realize that your law school years are foundational to the future "cathedral" that God wants to build in your life. It is a wrong mind-set to be thinking only about what you can do to *pass* an exam or *pass* the First-Year Law Students' Exam. Oak Brook students should not have a *passing* mentality, but they should have an *excelling* attitude. This requires consistent and diligent study as well as in-depth examination preparation and practice.

When you reach the time to prepare for examinations, you should be at the point where you are familiar with the substantive law and are working with the material to comprehend its various implications and applications. This can be done in several ways, a combination of which, is the best way to prepare for exams. Using flash cards that give you a question in the context of a factual setting, reviewing multiple-choice questions, and writing out answers to essay questions all increase your comprehension and your ability to apply the subject matter in a course.

IRAC (Issue, Rule, Application, and Conclusion)

The primary method of analysis you should use in examinations is the IRAC method. You will soon realize that this is the same type of analysis judges usually use in writing their opinions, and it is also the same analysis that you should use in writing case briefs. Using this analysis as you write briefs and read cases will greatly prepare you to use it in exams.

Memorizing definitions and rules of law is necessary and very important, because they will help you spot the *issues* in an examination question. Whether it is an essay question or a multiple-choice test, spotting issues is critical because it is always the first step in your analysis. If you know these definitions and rules, including the exceptions to the rules, you will be able to determine if the facts omit, distort, or add to what is necessary to comply with the legal definitions or rules that you have studied and memorized. For example, if the facts state that John said, "I would like to buy your house," you should see that the first issue in a contracts question is whether John's words constitute an offer. Knowing the definition of an offer and the required elements will enable you to spot the offer issue.

Memorizing definitions and rules is not only necessary to spot issues, but it is also the next step in the analysis: *rule*. After you state what the issue is, you should then state the general rule that applies. Through your study of cases and other materials, you will learn what rules apply to what issues. For example, you will receive no credit if you apply the rules regarding the Statute of Frauds to a situation where there is an oral contract for cutting grass for one summer. Even if you state the rules correctly, if they do not apply, you will show that you really did not understand the rules. You will also demonstrate your current inexperience in legal analysis.

In the *rule* portion of your analysis, you articulate the rule that is applicable to the issue. After stating the rule, you should apply the facts to the rule to decide if the facts stated include all the necessary elements of the relevant definitions or rules. In the above example about John, the rule is that an offer is a manifestation of present contractual intent communicated to the offeree in sufficiently definite terms. The terms must include quantity, time of performance, identity of the parties, price, and subject matter. The *application* portion discusses whether John's statement was sufficient to be a legal offer. While it was a statement of John's interest, it was not sufficient to constitute an offer, because there was no price term or communication of the time of performance.

The above example is a very simple example of the application part of the analysis, but it demonstrates how important it is to arrive at the correct legal *conclusion*. Inserting the facts into the definition or the rule helps you see if the legal issue is to be decided in the negative (i.e., the answer to the issue is no), or whether the correct conclusion is that the issue is to be decided in the positive. In the above example, the conclusion is that John's statement does not constitute an offer because it contains neither the element of price nor the time of performance.

Obviously, examination questions contain many issues, and your success on an examination depends on your ability to spot the issues and analyze them correctly, using the correct rules of law to reach the right legal conclusion. Simply spotting the issues will not get you full credit on an exam question. Professors, Bar examiners, judges, and clients want to see analysis and conclusions as well. Even in a multiple-choice exam, the same skills of analysis are necessary. The question asked directly or indirectly raises the legal issue, and you must discern which facts are relevant to the issue and decide which answer states the best legal conclusion based upon the law you studied. Practice is the only way to gain these skills. Your law school success and your success as a minister of reconciliation and justice depends largely upon developing these skills.

Adversarial Method of Analysis

In examinations and also in the real legal world, there are often no clear answers. Even if you use the correct IRAC analysis, it still may be difficult to reach a solid legal conclusion. This is when you include the adversarial analysis in answering questions. If the issue is difficult to decide because there are facts supporting both a negative and a positive resolution, you should discuss both sides. In the discussion, you would describe both the strengths and weaknesses of each side's position. After discussing both sides of an argument, you should then decide which position you think is the better one, and state your reasons for the conclusion. Always arrive at a conclusion in your answer to an essay question, even if it is a tentative one.

Multiple-choice questions often require you to work through the adversarial analysis before you can choose the best answer. It is understood in such questions that there really is no "right" answer, but only one that is legally more defensible. The skill of seeing both sides of an issue is essential in doing well on examinations and can be mastered only after becoming competent in the IRAC analysis. Regardless of which side of an issue one argues, that side must use the IRAC analysis to support its position. If IRAC is not used within the adversarial analysis, the discussion degenerates to only a debate on differing opinions that are not rooted in legal logic. Examination answers including language like "I think A should win because it is the right thing" will get you few points from a professor.

Approach for Different Subjects

Students soon learn that the way to respond to a contracts essay question is different from both a torts or a criminal law essay question. The reason for the differences involves the number and type of issues. With a contracts question, the overriding issue is whether there has been a breach of an enforceable contract. The cause of action is always breach of contract or a request for equitable relief. But within this issue or cause of action, there are many sub-issues that are related and dependent upon each other. It is like going down a road with many forks in the road. The fork you take will determine your ultimate conclusion. The answer to each sub-issue is the building block for the next sub-issue.

A party will never recover for contractual damages unless there was a valid contract or unless there was reasonable detrimental reliance on the part of the plaintiff. By using the IRAC analysis, a student must first determine whether there was a valid offer, then whether the offer was revoked, then whether the offer was accepted, then whether there was consideration; if no consideration, then whether there was promissory estoppel, then whether there were any defenses to formation or enforcement, then whether there were any third-party rights involved, then whether there were any conditions involved, then whether there were any duties that were not discharged, then whether there was a breach, and then whether there were any damages. Only after addressing each of these issues (when relevant) have you properly answered a contracts final examination essay question.

With torts and criminal law, however, there are many different issues or causes of action that may be in the facts of a question. In a torts essay question, you may have facts that raise a negligence claim, a strict liability claim, a third-party liability claim, an intentional tort claim, an infliction of mental distress claim, and so on. Each of these claims has separate elements and should be separately analyzed using IRAC. For example, after you examined whether there is a negligence claim by discussing whether there was a duty, breach of duty, causation, and damages, the discussion about negligence is over. You would then discuss another cause of action in tort, such as strict liability if it was relevant, and complete that analysis by discussing the elements in this tort.

You can see that each tort cause of action is separate and distinct from the others, even though each cause of action arises out of the same facts. If you are unable to discuss completely one tort issue or cause of action, it does not affect your ability to discuss another tort issue or cause of action because they are unrelated to each other.

Each has its own separate elements, which must be satisfied to justify recovery of money damages.

The analysis for a criminal law question is very similar to that of torts in that there are many different crimes that could arise out of the same factual situation. One person could be charged with several crimes and there could be several people involved in the facts. This requires a discussion of each crime (its definition and elements) for which each person could be charged. Plus, the fact that there is more than one person involved would probably require a discussion of conspiracy and accomplice principles. For example, the same person could be charged with assault, battery, burglary, and rape if the facts supported such a conclusion. Each of these charges would need to be discussed separately, because they are not related to each other.

Because of the number and the distinctiveness of the issues in torts and criminal law exam questions, time may not permit the same depth of discussion expected in a contracts exam. Obviously, the more complete your discussion on an issue, the more points you will earn on that issue. However, in a torts or criminal law exam, it is a serious mistake to take so much time on one or two issues that you never discuss the others. Torts and criminal law professors want to see that you spotted all the causes of actions or crimes and are able to discuss (at least to a minimum degree) the elements of each—as applied to the facts—to reach a conclusion. If time is running out, it is better to show the professor that you spotted an issue and only discuss it minimally than to discuss some issues thoroughly but fail to even mention others.

The same exam-taking strategy applies to contracts exams as well, but because of the interrelationship of the issues, a more detailed discussion is generally required to support your conclusion on one issue, which is the basis for your discussion of the next issue. The difference in the required discussion between contracts and criminal law exams or torts exams also affects the format of your answers. It is always good to use headings in your essay and to discuss the issue in a logical IRAC format. The more you can write in a cohesive essay format the better. The First-Year Law Students' Exam examiners want to see "evidence of your ability to apply the law to the given facts and to reason in a logical, lawyer-like manner from the premises you adopt to a sound conclusion." Your professors want to see the same thing.

The differences in the expectations of your professors are due more to the nature of the subject matter than to any differences in the type of essays that are desirable. As was previously mentioned, the number of issues in a criminal law or torts essay question could be so great that more of an outline format is necessary because of time. Your professor understands this and would rather have an outline of all the issues than a thorough discussion of only a few. Probably the best way to help you understand how to approach essay questions is to give you examples of past midterm exams.

Sample Midterm Essay Questions

Midterm exams are designed to test your understanding of the subject matter studied up to that point in a course. They also give you the opportunity to demonstrate the skills you have learned in identifying relevant facts, issues, and applicable law. The goal in answering essay questions is to respond to the "call of the question" and to do so in a way that shows your understanding of the subject matter and your ability to think and write in a logical and coherent manner.

Following are past midterm essay questions in torts, criminal law, and contracts. Each question is followed with discussion on how to approach writing a good answer using the IRAC method and, when appropriate, the adversarial method of analysis.

Torts

Midterm Essay Question

While passing through New England on a recent vacation, Paul and Ashley Smith, along with their five children, stopped for dinner at the historic Publick House Inn (where George Washington once dined and slept many years ago). Because of the size of their family, they were seated in a private room containing a long table, a fireplace, and colonial-style furniture, including a tall cupboard in the corner. On the first shelf of this cupboard sat a large bowl containing many chocolates. This candy belonged to the Smith's waitress, Denise, who had placed the candy in the bowl at the beginning of her work shift and who was intending to share it with the other staff members during a staff party at the end of the shift.

Almost immediately after being seated in this room, mischievous Michael, the Smith's five-year-old son, began to roam around the room, and he discovered the chocolates. As was his practice at all of the banks, businesses, and restaurants he visited that had complimentary candy bowls, Michael began to rip into Denise's candy, stuffing his mouth and pockets with great rapidity and glee. Paul and Ashley were tired from the long day, and they were somewhat preoccupied with trying to read the extensive menu, so they chose to overlook Michael's pillage of the candy bowl.

After much ado, dinner was ordered, and Denise began to serve the main course to the family. While serving a side order of beets to Ashley, Denise accidentally splashed some beet juice on Ashley's white sweater. Ashley knew she would never be able to get all of the stain out of the sweater, but she hurried off to the restroom to clean up as much as possible.

At about the same time, Paul realized that he had not washed his hands, so he hurried off to the men's room, which happened to be in the basement below the dining room and down a winding hallway. Halfway down this curious hallway was a small, wooden door framed by an arched opening cut into the stone-and-mortar foundation wall. On this door was a small sign that read, "Employees Only." The sign piqued Paul's interest even more, so he pushed on the door and it creaked open. He crouched down and passed through the small opening, and to his delight found himself in a dark, cool, musty room. He began exploring, feeling this and bumping into that, when a large bat suddenly flapped off of its perch and flew right for Paul's face. Paul quickly straightened up to avoid the bat, which caused his forehead to become impaled by a nail protruding from the low ceiling. Blood began gushing down his face and he made his way out of the room and headed for the manager's office.

Just as Denise was serving the last plates to the Smith family, she caught a glimpse of her candy bowl and saw that it was nearly empty. She was aghast and immediately began scanning the room to see if she could spot the culprit(s). She fixed her gaze on Michael. She quickly approached him and angrily asked, "You took my candy, didn't you?" He turned his head toward her and responded, "Who, me?" Denise detected a strong odor of chocolate on his breath and concluded that she had found her man. She grabbed his arm and dragged him down to the manager's office, despite his crying and pleas for mercy.

Denise held crying Michael in the manager's reception area for less than a minute before both Paul and Ashley stormed in—Paul holding his bleeding head and Ashley holding a very stained sweater. The manager then entered, introduced himself, and listened as everyone quickly told their stories. The manager then ducked into his office, took two aspirin, and called you for some legal advice. From a torts point of view, write what you would have told the manager regarding all of the torts that occurred, the parties involved, and the possible outcomes of each.

Discussion of Torts Essay Question

After reading the facts of the question, you must make sure that you clearly understand the call of the question. Students often miss points because they fail to answer part of what was asked or they write things that are not responsive to the call of the question.

In this problem, the call involves three main elements: the parties, the claims, and the outcome of each claim. This really gives you the approach that you should use. First, identify the parties and which ones have claims against another. Second, discuss all of the possible legal claims that one party has against another. (This needs to be done for each plaintiff v. defendant combination.) Third, use the IRAC analysis to arrive at a conclusion on the outcome of each claim, including an adversarial discussion when the result is not clear.

The parties mentioned in the facts are: Paul, Ashley, Michael, Denise, and the Publick House Inn. It does not matter in what order you proceed, but you should begin by asking yourself the question, Which one of these parties has a tort claim against another one? For example, does Paul have a claim against any other party? Based upon your knowledge of the facts and the law, you would know that Paul has a claim against Publick House, but Publick House also has a claim (counterclaim) against Paul. You would then discuss all the claims Paul has against Publick House (Paul v. Publick House), and in a separate discussion you would analyze the counterclaim Publick House has against Paul.

In each of your plaintiff/defendant discussions, you would articulate the claims, the defenses, and the likely outcome of the dispute. Of course, you should include a discussion of every possible claim each party could bring. This is why it is so important to know the numerous causes of actions in tort law, the elements of each, and the defenses.

Your professor is looking to see how many of the claims you identify and how well you discuss each claim. Many professors use a checklist to evaluate a student's success in spotting the issues. The number of points given for each issue depends upon the quality and accuracy of the discussion. The following is a checklist for the above essay question.

Point Checklist

Paul v. Publick House	
Negligence for impaling head	10
Duty (no duty owed to trespasser)	
Strict liability for bat	10
Lack of ownership of bat	

Publick House v. Paul	
Trespass to land	5
Landowner duty (invitee to trespasser, to invitee)	2
Denise v. Michael	
Conversion (taking candy)	5
Implied consent possible defense	
Michael v. Denise and Publick House	
Assault	5
Battery	5
Intentional infliction of emotional distress	5
False imprisonment	5
Detention for investigation	
Vicarious liability	15
Denise v. Paul and Ashley	
Parents' liability for torts of children	3
Ashley v. Denise and Publick House	
Vicarious liability	15
Negligence in dumping beets	15
Duty	
Breach	
Causation	
Damages	

You can see that a torts essay question normally involves many claims and several parties. Not all the causes of actions are worth the same point value. Through practice you will be able to discern which issues are more important than others. Usually, greater point value is given to the more complex issues. Some claims are more likely to succeed than others, but on an exam you will want to discuss as many as you can.

Now that you understand the general approach to the question and have seen the point checklist, it will be helpful to look at a sample answer written by a student. In order to save time, notice that headings are used to identify the *issue* and definitions are used to state the *rule* to be applied. The discussion includes *application* of the law to the facts to reach the *conclusion*. This sample answer would be considered a good answer, if done under normal exam conditions with only one hour to respond.

Paul v. Publick House

Negligence

A breach of duty which actually and proximately causes injury to the person or property of another.

Duty

Invitee

An invitee is one who is invited onto the owner/occupier's land to fulfill a business objective of the owner/occupier. A landowner owes a duty to make a reasonable inspection of the premises and to correct or warn of any dangerous conditions, which a reasonable inspection would reveal.

Paul will argue that because he was a paying guest at the House, he was an invitee and the House owed him a duty to inspect the premises for any dangerous conditions, which a reasonable inspection would reveal. However, Paul was not an invitee to that part of the inn.

Trespasser

A trespasser is someone who comes onto the owner/occupier's land without permission. A landowner owes no duty to an unknown trespasser.

House will rebut that Paul was an invitee. A person's status can change. When Paul went through the door marked "Employees Only," he became a trespasser because he was not an employee.

Therefore, House will not be liable for negligence, because Paul became a trespasser by going through that door and, as such, House owed him no duty and he cannot recover.

Strict Liability

A person is strictly liable for injuries caused by animals in his possession.

Paul may argue that the bat caused his injury, because if it were not for the bat, he would not have moved to avoid the bat (which was flying towards him), and he would not have hit his head. However, the facts do not indicate that the bat belonged to Publick House. Further, it is questionable whether the type of injury Paul received was foreseeable.

Therefore, it is not likely that Paul could recover from Publick House under a strict liability theory.

Publick House v. Paul

Trespass to Land

The intentional entry upon land in possession of another without consent or privilege.

When Paul went behind the door marked "Employees Only," there was an entry upon another's land, because even though Paul had permission to be at Publick House, he did not have permission to go into that room. Furthermore, Paul was conscious that he was not an employee but still intended to go through the door.

Therefore, even though Paul initially had permission to be on the land, he will be liable for trespass to land because he went past the door marked "Employees Only."

Denise v. Michael

Conversion

The intentional wrongful exercise of dominion and control over chattel in possession of another without consent or privilege.

When Michael ate the candy, there was a wrongful exercise of dominion over Denise's candy because she was dispossessed of her candy. Furthermore, Michael's act was intentional because he intended to eat the candy even though he did not know he was not supposed to eat it. Mistake of fact will not negate intent.

Defense

Implied Consent

Michael may argue that he did not intend to take Denise's candy but that he thought the candy was for those who wanted it: he believed it was complimentary (as in other places) and that therefore, there was consent. But this defense is weak because of the location of the candy. It was not in a place readily accessible to the public.

Therefore, Michael will be liable for conversion.

Michael v. Denise and Publick House

Vicarious Liability

Respondeat Superior: A master is vicariously liable for the torts of his servants that occur within the course and scope of their employment.

Denise was employed by Publick House and, as such, was its servant. Therefore, Publick House will be liable for those torts committed by Denise within the course and scope of her employment.

Assault

The intentional placing of another in reasonable apprehension of an imminent, harmful or offensive touching.

When Denise approached Michael and grabbed him, it is likely that Michael saw her coming and was placed in apprehension of a touching. Denise intended to grab Michael. Further, he did not consent.

Defense

Recapture of Chattel

Denise may assert that she was seeking to recapture her chocolates that were for the party later that evening. However, a court will probably find that her means of recovery was not reasonable. Therefore, this defense will fail.

Therefore, Denise will be liable for assault.

Battery

The intentional harmful or offensive touching of another without consent or privilege.

When Denise grabbed Michael's arm, at least an offensive touching occurred. Denise's act was intentional, and Michael did not consent to this touching.

Therefore, Denise will be liable for battery.

Intentional Infliction of Emotional Distress

Conduct of an outrageous nature, which intentionally or recklessly causes severe emotional distress.

When Denise angrily approached Michael and then dragged him to the manager's office, it is arguable that her conduct was outrageous since Michael was only five years old. Further, as a result of Denise's actions, Michael began crying and pleading for mercy. Thus, it is arguable that for his age it was very traumatic and he suffered severe emotional distress.

It is possible that Denise may be held liable for intentional infliction of emotional distress. More facts would need to be known to make this determination.

False Imprisonment

The intentional physical or psychological confinement of another without consent or privilege.

When Denise dragged Michael by the arm and kept him in the manager's reception area, she physically confined him, even though it was only for a minute. Michael was aware of this confinement. Further, Michael did not consent to this confinement.

Defense

Detention for Investigation

Denise may assert that she had a privilege to take Michael for questioning concerning her missing chocolates. However, this privilege is usually limited to shopkeepers, thus this defense will probably fail because the chocolates were hers—they did not belong to the place in which she worked.

Therefore, Denise will likely be liable for false imprisonment.

Denise v. Paul and Ashley

Parents' Liability

Parents may not be held vicariously liable for the torts of their children. However, they may be held liable for their own negligence. Here, Denise may argue that Paul and Ashley were negligent in watching over Michael and making sure he did not get the candies. If she can prove that they were negligent, they may be held directly liable.

Ashley v. Denise and Publick House

Vicarious Liability

Defined above.

Because Denise was an employee of Publick House, Publick House will be vicariously liable for the torts Denise committed within the course and scope of her employment.

Negligence

A breach of duty, which actually and proximately causes injury to the person or property of another.

Duty

Denise had a duty to act as a reasonable waitress under the circumstances. Further, Denise had a special duty to come to Ashley's aid after she spilled the juice on Ashley's sweater because she had caused Ashley's peril.

Breach

Ashley may assert that Denise breached this duty when she spilled beet juice on Ashley's white sweater. However, this was an accident. Denise will argue that the reasonable person is not perfect. Unless Ashley can show that Denise was acting unreasonably when she spilled the juice, it would not be considered a breach.

However, Ashley will at least be able to prove that Denise breached her duty to come to Ashley's aid. After Denise spilled the beet juice on Ashley, Denise did not help her clean it up. Therefore, a court will probably find that there was a breach of Denise's duty.

Causation

But for Denise spilling the beet juice and failing to help clean it off Ashley's sweater, the sweater would not have been stained. Furthermore, the damage was a reasonably foreseeable consequence of Denise's negligence. The damage was the direct cause and the proximate cause of Denise's negligence.

Damages

Ashley will be able to recover general damages for her stained sweater.

Criminal Law

Midterm Essay Question

Dias believed his marriage to Deborah was going well; however, Deborah kept telling him that something was wrong. In November, Deborah decided she wanted a divorce. She asked her sister, Karen, to help move Dias's personal items out of the house while he was at work. Deborah had the house locks changed to prevent Dias from entering after the divorce papers were served. During the next two months, Deborah continued to have contact with Dias. On one occasion he struck Deborah with an ironing cord. Despite this incident, she made plans to see him over the holidays.

One of Dias's co-workers thought Dias and Deborah were trying to patch up their marriage. Two co-workers heard Dias say that if he had a gun, he would shoot his wife and then kill himself. Neither co-worker took him seriously. On New Year's Day, Deborah and Dias arranged to see each other. After giving her a bird as an anniversary present, Dias asked Deborah if she wanted to reconcile. Deborah said, "No." She further stated that she had already filed the divorce papers and did not want to get back together. Dias urged her to reconsider. According to Dias himself, he "lost it." At knifepoint, he took Deborah's new television set and stereo from her, placed them in his car, and locked them up.

Upon returning to the house, he immediately grabbed a knife from a butcher block in the kitchen but decided the knife was too small. He pulled out a large carving fork. Dias said, "Well Deb, this is it. I'm ending this right now." He told her that he could not live without her. Dias stabbed Deborah in the abdomen and chest. She fell to the ground screaming, "Why are you doing this?" Dias then stabbed Deborah in the leg. Dias then stabbed himself in the stomach as Deborah lay on the floor watching him self-inflict these wounds. Because he wanted Deborah to die, he held his hand over her mouth and nose to prevent her from breathing. Within a minute, Deborah made some guttural noises and then was silent. She was dead. With the fork still in him, Dias lay down beside her.

The next morning, Dias called 911 and said he had killed his wife and had stabbed himself. When the police arrived, they found Deborah's corpse in the kitchen. Dias was lying beside her. An autopsy revealed that "multiple, penetrating stab wounds to the chest and abdomen" caused Deborah's death. The coroner also found some hemorrhaging in Deborah's eye common to people who have died from asphyxiation.

Identify and fully discuss every crime that has been committed in the fact pattern and tell why you believe the crimes indicated have been committed. Please note: You must list the crimes committed in the order of their occurrence in the fact pattern. Failure to follow this instruction will result in a deduction of points.

Discussion of Criminal Law Essay Question

While it is not uncommon for criminal law questions to have multiple parties, this question has only one perpetrator and one victim. The call of the question focuses on the crimes committed. Therefore, all the analysis is under *State v. Dias*. Similar to tort questions containing many claims, criminal law questions usually have many independent crimes to discuss. Some crimes are lesser-included offenses of others, but each crime must be analyzed separately.

As with tort questions, the IRAC analysis is necessary with respect to each issue. Headings and definitions are commonly used to save time, but the response should remain an essay. Professors and Bar examiners look for coherent discussions that integrate the law and the facts to reach an accurate legal conclusion on each issue.

Point Checklist

Dias battery on Deb (ironing cord)	5
Dias assault on Deb (threatened gun incident)	2
Dias aggravated assault on Deb (knifepoint)	5
Dias possible false imprisonment/kidnapping	10
Dias aggravated robbery/larceny on Deb (TV, etc.)	10
Dias aggravated burglary on Deb (return to house)	10
Dias aggravated battery on Deb (stabbing/merger)	10
Dias murder of Deb	48

As previously stated, the approach and format to criminal law essay questions are very similar to that of torts. Independent causes of actions or claims can be discussed in any order. However, if one crime is a lesser-included offense in another, the lesser-included offense should be discussed first. Consider the following sample answer to the criminal law question above.

State v. Dias

Assault

An assault may be either a substantial step toward perpetration of an intended battery or the intentional placing of another in reasonable apprehension of imminent bodily harm.

When Dias struck Deborah with the ironing cord, he took a substantial step toward the perpetration of an intended battery.

Therefore, Dias was guilty of assault; however, the assault will merge into the battery.

Battery

Battery is the unlawful application of force to another's person, without consent or privilege.

When Dias struck Deborah with the ironing cord, there was an application of force to Deborah's person. Furthermore, because she did not consent and he had no justification for striking her, the force was unlawful.

Therefore, Dias will be guilty of battery.

Aggravated Assault

Aggravated assault: An assault carried out with a deadly weapon.

When Dias "lost it" and threatened Deborah at knifepoint, he placed her in apprehension of imminent harm. A knife is considered a deadly weapon and constitutes an aggravated assault.

Therefore, Dias will be guilty of aggravated assault.

Aggravated Robbery

Robbery is the trespassory taking of another's personal property from his person by violence or intimidation.

When Dias took Deborah's new television set and stereo and locked them in his car, a trespassory taking occurred because they belonged to Deborah and she did not consent. Dias took them from her at knifepoint; therefore, the taking was from her person by violence, or at least intimidation, because a knife is a deadly weapon.

Therefore, Dias will be guilty of aggravated robbery.

Aggravated Burglary

Common Law Burglary: The breaking and entering of a dwelling of another in the nighttime with the specific intent to commit a felony therein.

When Dias returned to Deborah's house after locking her items in his car, he entered her home. He had previously moved out, and the locks had been changed to prevent him from entering without her permission. Because he had just threatened Deborah at knife-point, it is unlikely that he had her consent to return.

The facts do not indicate whether there was a breaking. As long as Dias did not reenter through an already open door, there was most likely a breaking because he probably did not have permission to reenter. There are no facts indicating whether this occurred during the nighttime.

The state may assert that Dias had the requisite specific intent necessary for burglary. That is, he intended to commit a felony (murder) within Deborah's home. The state may claim that his intent was evidenced by his immediately grabbing a knife and by his prior statements to his co-workers. A court would probably find that Dias had the necessary *mens rea*.

Therefore, if Dias did not reenter the home through an open door and if the entering occurred at night, he will be guilty of Common Law burglary.

Modern Law Burglary: The trespassory entering of any structure with the intent to commit a crime therein.

As discussed above, Dias reentered Deborah's home. We can assume that he did not have permission to reenter, because this occurred immediately following his threatening her with a knife. Therefore, there was a trespassory entering.

Finally, a court will probably find that Dias had the requisite intent to commit a crime, that is, he intended to kill Deborah as evidenced by his actions and prior statements.

Therefore, at the very least, Dias will be guilty of modern law burglary.

False Imprisonment

False imprisonment is the unlawful confinement or detention of another.

The state may argue that when Dias took Deborah's belongings at knifepoint, she was unlawfully confined in her house. Further, the state may alternately argue that when Dias returned to Deborah's home and began stabbing and suffocating her, he prevented her from going anywhere by his use of force.

It is possible that Dias may be guilty of false imprisonment; however, this will probably be considered a lesser-included offense of either the robbery and/or murder and thus will merge.

Kidnapping

The intentional and unlawful movement of another.

As discussed above, Deborah may have been falsely imprisoned. However, there are no facts to indicate that Deborah was transported in any way. However, some modern statutes expand the definition of *kidnapping* to include false imprisonment when a deadly weapon is used.

Therefore, if the jurisdiction had a modern statute, Dias would be guilty of kidnapping. However, this will probably merge into the greater offense of murder.

Aggravated Battery

Battery, as defined above, is the unlawful application of force to another's person. When that force involves a deadly weapon, the battery becomes aggravated battery.

When Dias stabbed Deborah multiple times and then proceeded to cover her mouth and nose to prevent her from breathing, he unlawfully applied force to her person. A carving fork could be considered a deadly weapon, thus elevating the battery to aggravated battery.

Therefore, Dias will be guilty of aggravated battery. However, this will merge with the greater offense of murder.

Homicide

Homicide is the killing of a human being by another human being.

Deborah died as a result of the actions of Dias, both being human beings; therefore, a homicide has occurred.

Actual Cause

But for Dias stabbing Deborah and holding his hands over her mouth and nose, thereby suffocating her, Deborah would not have died.

Proximate Cause

It is foreseeable that stabbing someone and then preventing them from breathing, even if for a short period of time, could result in death.

Murder

Murder is the unlawful killing of another with malice aforethought. Malice can be shown by: (1) intent to kill, (2) intent to cause serious bodily injury, (3) felony murder rule, and (4) depraved heart act.

Intent to Kill

The state would argue that Dias intended to kill Deborah. His intent to kill was evidenced by several things. Dias had told his co-workers that if he had a gun, he would shoot his wife and then kill himself. When Dias reentered the home, he decided the first knife he had was too small, thus arguably evidencing his deliberation and intent. Finally, stabbing and suffocating someone usually results in that person's death, and his methods further evidenced his intent to kill her. The state will probably be able to prove intent to kill.

Intent to Cause Serious Bodily Injury

If, for some reason, the state is unable to prove intent to kill based on the above arguments, it will at least be able to prove that by stabbing Deborah repeatedly and preventing her from breathing, Dias intended to cause serious bodily injury to her.

Depraved Heart Act

At the very least, Dias's actions were performed in extreme recklessness for human life.

Felony Murder Rule

The state may further argue that the killing occurred during the commission of an inherently dangerous felony, that is, the burglary. However, this argument will probably fail, because the burglary was not independent of the murder. The state may further assert that it occurred shortly after the robbery, that the robbery was separate, and that Dias had never really reached a place of safety. It is questionable whether the court would apply the felony murder rule here.

First-Degree Murder

Murder by premeditation and deliberation, poison, bomb, ambush, torture, or during the commission of an enumerated felony.

The state will argue that Dias had premeditated the murder of Deborah as evidenced by his statements to his co-workers and his deliberation over which weapon to use. Furthermore, the state may assert that his stabbing Deborah multiple times and then preventing her from breathing was a form of torture. Finally, robbery is an enumerated felony; therefore, if the court finds the felony murder rule to apply, it may also work to convict Dias of first-degree murder.

A court will probably find Dias guilty of first-degree murder based on one of the above theories.

Second-Degree Murder

All other murders not raised to the first degree.

If the state is unable to prove first-degree murder, Dias will be guilty of at least second-degree murder based on a depraved heart killing.

Voluntary Manslaughter

Voluntary manslaughter is an intentional homicide committed with malice but with adequate provocation.

Dias may argue that he should not be guilty of murder because the homicide was a result of provocation. In order to mitigate the murder to manslaughter, Dias must have been provoked without having sufficient time to cool. Furthermore, the case must be such that a reasonable person would have been provoked and not had time to cool. Dias may assert that when Deborah stated there was no chance of their marriage being reconciled, he "lost it," and that a reasonable person would have also lost control. However, most courts hold that mere words are generally not enough to justify a person's loss of control.

The state will rebut that Dias had enough time to cool because he had time to commit a robbery and he also deliberated about what type of weapon to use, showing that he would have had time to cool off.

Therefore, it is unlikely that Dias will be able to mitigate his conviction to manslaughter.

Involuntary Manslaughter

Involuntary manslaughter is an unintentional homicide without malice, which can arise in one of three ways: (1) commission of an unlawful act, (2) intention to inflict non-serious bodily harm, or (3) criminal negligence.

As discussed above, Dias will probably be found guilty of first-degree murder. However, at the very least, Dias will be guilty of involuntary manslaughter.

Contracts

Midterm Essay Question

The American Boy Campers (ABC) were having their annual fund-raising campaign to raise money in order to purchase land to use for their outdoor activities. Elmer and Elma Fuddy heard about ABC's need for a large tract of land on which to conduct their camping expeditions. They were interested in the well-being of their community's young people. They called True P. Leader, director of ABC, about whether ABC would be interested in land that Elmer and Elma owned.

After the telephone call, Elmer and Elma wrote a letter to True P. Leader, dated August 30, 2000, part of which stated: "We think the world of ABC. We want ABC to have our land of 300 acres, bordered by U.S. Highway 2 and County Road Q, known as Fuddy Woods. We hope this meets your fund-raising goal for this year. We would like to have the campsite named after us."

The letter went on to tell how ABC could start using the property in October. After their signatures, the Fuddys stated, "Before we convey the land, we ask that you finally pay the $2,000 for the grandfather clock that you had me make for your wife's birthday five years ago!"

All of those at ABC were excited about reaching their goal so quickly. True P. Leader sent a letter to Mr. and Mrs. Fuddy thanking them for the land, along with the check of $2,000 for the grandfather clock and a deed for the Fuddys to sign to convey the land. True P. Leader sent out notices that ABC had reached their fund-raising goal and that their fund-raising campaign was ending early. Elmer and Elma cashed the check, but they never signed the deed.

October came and ABC started clearing the land in preparation for their fall activities. ABC put in nature trails throughout much of the woods, built shower and toilet facilities, and dredged a pond for a swimming area. Membership in the ABC grew because of the new campground.

Sadly, Elmer Fuddy passed away on November 12, and Elma was faced with extra medical expenses and funeral bills. The only way that she could pay her bills would be for her to sell some of the ABC land.

Elma called True P. Leader and told him her situation. True P. Leader thought it would be a good example to the boys if they sold enough land to cover her bills, so he offered to sell ten acres. However, Elma said that the land was hers and that she needed all of the land in order to pay her bills and have some retirement income. True P. Leader said that he could not do that and that ABC had a right to the land.

Elma claims that there is no contract with ABC and that since she and her husband never signed the deed, she has the right to the property.

True P. Leader contacts you and wants legal counsel about the situation. Discuss the legal rights of the parties and the likely results of any litigation.

Discussion of Contracts Essay Question

One of the significant differences between contracts questions and questions in either torts or criminal law is that an initial determination of what principles of law will apply must be made. The law or rules that must be applied to a contracts question depend upon whether the subject matter of the contract is *goods*. If the subject matter is not goods, Common Law principles of contract law will be applied. If the subject matter is goods, the provisions of the Uniform Commercial Code (UCC) will control. The UCC sections that deal with the sale of goods have been adopted by every state and therefore cannot be ignored.

The decision whether to apply Common Law principles or UCC law is the first fork in the road in answering a contracts essay question. There are other decision points in answering a contracts question that determine the next step in your legal analysis of any given fact pattern. For example, you need to decide if a valid offer has been made. If the answer is yes, you would go on to a certain next step, but if the answer is no, you would go to a different next step. The decision you make obviously affects the rest of your entire answer to the question.

Because each step in analyzing a contracts essay question is the foundation for the next step, a student's answer can be derailed at any point along the track if a wrong decision is made at any fork in the road.

As you read the following sample answer to the American Boy Campers' question, it should be easy to see how contracts essays are much different than torts or criminal law essays. There are not independent causes of action that can be analyzed separately from each other, as there are in tort claims or crimes. There are separate issues, but they are all related to the one major issue in every contracts question: whether there has been a breach of contract for which one party can recover damages.

ABC v. Elma

UCC

This situation involves real estate, not the sale of goods. Therefore, Common Law principles of contract will govern the rights of the parties involved, not UCC rules.

Preliminary Considerations

If ABC has any rights in this situation, it will be by virtue of a contract or on the basis of quasi-contractual relief. In order for there to be a contract, there must be an offer, acceptance, and consideration. Also, there must be no valid defenses to formation of the contract or to its enforcement.

Offer

An offer is an outward manifestation of present contractual intent which is definite in terms and communicated in such a way as to create in the offeree a reasonable expectation that the offeror is willing to enter into a contract. Under the Common Law, an offer must be definite as to quantity, time of performance, identification of parties, price, and subject matter.

Did Elmer and Elma make an offer to ABC?

The letter Elmer and Elma wrote clearly expressed their intention to give the property to ABC. The quantity was stated (300 acres), the time of performance was given (October), the parties were identified, and the subject matter is land. The problem is that no price was given, unless the $2,000 requested for the grandfather clock can be considered a price.

ABC could argue that the language "Before we convey the land, we ask that you finally pay the $2,000 . . ." set a price, because it seems to indicate that the transfer is conditioned upon the payment of the money. But Elma would argue that the $2,000 was a personal debt of True P. Leader, not of ABC, and therefore could not be considered a price for the land. This would be true because the letter clearly stated that the $2,000 was for the grandfather clock.

Because the price element is missing, there is not a sufficient offer based upon Common Law rules. However, that does not mean that ABC will not be able to enforce the Fuddys' gift promise as is explained below.

Acceptance

An acceptance is an outward manifestation of unequivocal assent to the terms of an offer. Acceptance can be by words or actions in most cases.

Did ABC accept what Elmer and Elma offered?

The letter that True Leader sent was clearly an acceptance of the property offered. The letter thanked Elmer and Elma for the property and also enclosed a deed for the Fuddys to sign, plus a $2,000 check for the grandfather clock.

Consideration

Consideration is the bargained-for exchange of something of legal value between the parties. It is what induces the parties to act.

Was there consideration here?

It is clear that the Fuddys wanted to donate the property. They were not negotiating a price in exchange for the land. There was no bargained-for exchange and therefore there was no consideration.

The $2,000 was not for the land, and the request to have the campsite named after the Fuddys is not of legal value.

Consideration Substitute

Sometimes the courts will enforce the promise of a party, even when there is no consideration, if the promisor makes a promise that he reasonably foresees will induce the promisee to act or forbear to act in some way because of the promise, and the promisee does act or forebears to act. This is called *promissory estoppel.* In such situations, the court will enforce the promise to the extent necessary to prevent injustice (Restatement 2d 90).

If there is a promise to make a gift to a nonprofit organization (charity) such as the Boy Scouts or a University, there is a special rule that courts have applied to enforce a promise to make a gift to the recipient. It is the charitable subscription rule. Under this rule, the promise will be enforced even without proof that the promise induced action or forbearance.

In this situation, it was reasonable to foresee that the promise of the Fuddys would induce ABC to act or forebear to act. In fact, ABC did act upon the promise. They cancelled the remainder of the fund-raising drive and made many improvements on the property in preparation to use it. Therefore, there is good reason to enforce the promise to prevent injustice.

Defenses

Because there was no consideration or price element, the facts do not support a view that there was a contract. Lack of consideration is a defense to formation, and Elma would be successful in her argument that there was no contract.

If there were no defenses to formation, there still would be a possible defense to enforcement: the Statute of Frauds. Contracts involving an interest in land is one of the categories of contracts that must be in writing to be enforceable. There are several ways to satisfy the Statute of Frauds requirement even though there is no formal written agreement. One way is by a sufficient memorandum. If there is any writing, signed by the party to be charged (i.e., the defendant, in this case, the Fuddys) that reasonably identifies the subject matter, is sufficient to indicate that a contract has been made between the parties, and states with reasonable certainty the essential terms of any unperformed promises, it will satisfy the Statute of Frauds. The writing can be a combination of writings constituting the offer and acceptance.

In this case, ABC could make a good argument that the two letters between the parties would satisfy the Statute of Frauds.

Another way to satisfy the Statute is by part performance, or in this case, occupation with apparent permission. ABC has good evidence that there was an agreement, because they occupied the land in October and began making substantial preparations for the fall activities. Generally, people do not participate in such activity on land unless there is some agreement with the owner.

Conclusion

Based upon this analysis, there is no contract between the Fuddys and ABC. On this point, Elma would win. However, because of the concepts of *promissory estoppel* and the charitable subscription rule, ABC would be able to enforce the promise, at least to the degree necessary to prevent injustice. Because of the reliance made upon the promise by ABC, it is likely that the court would rule that ABC would be able to retain the property necessary for its operations. Elma would probably be able to recover the remainder of the land. She would probably be ordered to convey only that amount of land necessary to meet the original goals of ABC. Therefore, ABC is in a good position, but will not likely be able to keep all 300 acres of the land.

The point values for the above question are below.

UCC and preliminary considerations	5
Offer	20
Acceptance	10
Consideration	10
Consideration substitute/charitable subscription	25
Defenses	20
Conclusion/damages	10

Additional Examples

As you can see, responding to essay examination questions is practice for the real-world situations when you begin to practice law. A client will come in and tell his or her story. You, as the legal counselor, will need to be able to distinguish the legally relevant facts from the commentary. Oftentimes, it will be necessary to ask many questions to obtain the information you need. You will also need to discern the true legal issues so you can apply the applicable law to reach a preliminary legal conclusion.

As with any skill, competence requires study, application, and practice. Writing answers to essay questions is no different. Diligent effort will surely bear fruit. To give you more instruction and practice in writing answers to essay questions, examples of final exam questions are included in the Appendix.

Conclusion

The study of law is a challenging and fulfilling endeavor. No matter how long one practices law, the study continues. Training in the law provides one with skills applicable to many areas of life. Whether it is within business, family, church, or government, legal training helps one to be a more fruitful servant. That is the goal! As Christians, each of us should view the study of law as preparation to fulfill the calling God has placed upon our lives. After seeing the current and potential strongholds in legal study, you must seek God and study His Word to renew your mind, and you must put on the character of Christ so that you will be equipped to be a faithful and profitable servant. It will not be you, but it will be Christ working through you!

APPENDIX

SAMPLE FINAL EXAM ESSAY QUESTIONS

TORTS

Final Exam Essay Question

Billy Bongo was director of Camp Candy, a summer resort campground that catered exclusively to rich kids. The camp was located in a humid, tropical climate surrounded by a swamp on one side and a jungle on the other, making it a very attractive environment for mosquitoes. During a particularly pesky and aggravating mosquito season three years ago, Billy Bongo purchased a two-ounce bottle of Mosquito Drop Dead body lotion from the local shopping channel and used it with satisfactory results.

Billy was so satisfied with the mosquito lotion that he purchased 1,000 gallons of the substance from the local shopping channel for use at Camp Candy. Billy hired Flyer Ned, a local farmer/crop duster, to fly all over his camp, spraying the lotion in an effort to curb the mosquito population.

Unbeknownst to Flyer Ned or Billy Bongo, Mosquito Drop Dead body lotion contained a high concentration of ethyl zylonene, a substance that is highly combustible in its wet state but once dried, is perfectly harmless. Unfortunately, as Ned began to spray the lotion from an altitude of 300 feet, it was sucked into the intake manifold of his HighFlyer 300Z (manufactured by Wing and a Prayer Airplane Co.), causing the vapor to instantly combust. The combustion of the ethyl zylonene caused the engine of the airplane to accelerate at a high rate of speed, which in turn created a stronger suction, causing more ethyl zylonene to be sucked into the engine. The plane kept accelerating until the wings of the airplane came apart due to the stress of the high speeds. Flyer Ned jumped from the runaway plane and parachuted to safety.

Wing and a Prayer Airplane Co. failed to employ any sort of filtering system on the HighFlyer 300Z, even though approximately 50% of other airplane manufacturers employed such a device.

Fortunately, the bug lotion successfully killed off every mosquito within 25 miles of Camp Candy, but unfortunately, the runaway airplane eventually crashed into Zippy (Farmer Fran's valuable stud bull), killing him instantly.

Flyer Ned was charged with violating the FAA's maximum speed limit for the altitude at which he was flying.

Discuss the tort rights and liabilities of all parties.

Good Answer

Farmer Fran v. Flyer Ned

Trespass to Land

The intentional entry upon land in possession of another without consent or privilege.

When the plane crashed on Fran's property, there was an entry upon another's land. When Ned jumped out of the plane, he knew it would land somewhere. Therefore, a court may find that he had sufficient intent even though he may not have specifically intended for it to land on Fran's property.

However, Ned will be able to argue the defense of private necessity. If this defense works, he will not be liable for trespass to land, but he will still have to pay for the damage he caused to Fran's property.

Conversion

Fran's valuable stud bull was killed as a result of the plane crashing into it. Therefore, Fran was dispossessed of her chattel. A court will probably find intent as discussed above. However, Ned will be able to assert private necessity as a defense.

Ned will probably not be liable for conversion, though he will have to pay damages for the death of the bull.

Negligence

A breach of duty, which actually and proximately causes injury to the person or property of another.

Ned owed a duty to act as a reasonable person. Fran may argue that Ned breached his duty by negligently flying and by jumping from the plane. However, a reasonable person would probably have abandoned the runaway plane and not stayed. Therefore, Ned probably did not breach his duty.

Negligence Per Se

Ned violated the statute by going over the maximum speed limit. Fran will argue that this should establish a breach by Ned of his duty.

Farmer Fran v. Camp Candy

Vicarious Liability

A master is vicariously liable for the torts of his servants that occur within the course and scope of their employment.

Ned was hired by Camp Candy. However, he had his own plane and was not under the supervision of Camp. Therefore, he will probably be found to be an independent contractor rather than an employee and thus Camp should not be liable. To refute this, Fran will claim that spraying the lotion was dangerous and thus a non-delegable duty.

Flyer Ned v. Billy

Negligence

Defined above.

Ned may argue that Billy was negligent in not finding out whether it was safe to spray the product over the camp and in providing dangerous chemicals to Ned because a reasonable person would have inquired about the ingredients and investigated the effect of spraying the lotion. Therefore, Billy breached his duty.

Further, Ned's injury, that is, the loss of his plane, would not have happened but for Billy giving him a substance to spray that was highly combustible. Further, it is foreseeable that not checking to make sure a chemical is safe to spray could result in injury to people. Billy may argue that the defective plane was an intervening cause. However, this will probably fail.

Ned suffered damages because his plane crashed.

Contributory Negligence

In some jurisdictions, a plaintiff will be barred from recovery for negligence if it can be shown that he negligently contributed to his own injury.

Billy will argue that Ned was contributorily negligent in not inquiring as to whether the product was safe. Since he was a farmer/crop duster, he should have had more reason to be aware of the possible harm.

Comparative Negligence

In some jurisdictions, a plaintiff's claim for recovery will be reduced by the amount that he negligently contributed to his own injury.

If Billy can show contributory negligence, Ned's recovery will depend on what jurisdiction they live in.

Assumption of the Risk

Ned did not voluntarily assume the risk since he did not know that the lotion would cause the plane to accelerate and the wings to come apart.

Ned v. Camp Candy

Vicarious Liability

Defined above.

Billy was the director of Camp Candy. Therefore, he is their servant and they will be vicariously liable for any torts committed by Billy within the course and scope of his employment.

Flyer Ned v. Shopping Channel

Strict Products Liability

When manufacturers or distributors of goods place a product that is defective and unreasonably dangerous into the stream of commerce, they will be held strictly liable for damages resulting from the use of the defective product.

Ned may claim that the product was unreasonably dangerous because it caused the plane to accelerate above the normal rate. However, Shopping will counter that the substance was not unreasonably dangerous in its normal use and that it was a body lotion, not meant to be sprayed from planes, and that if the product had been used properly it would not have been dangerous at all.

Furthermore, Ned's misuse of the product caused his injury, and such misuse was not foreseeable. Therefore, Shopping will probably not be liable for strict products liability because the product was not unreasonably dangerous.

Flyer Ned v. Wing and Prayer

Negligent Products Liability

When a manufacturer of goods places a product into the stream of commerce, it owes a duty to conduct a reasonable inspection of the product and to correct or warn of any dangerous defects, which a reasonable inspection would reveal.

If Ned can show that the risk of harm outweighed the utility of not having a filter on the plane, and that the plane was below the standard of the industry, Ned may be able to prove that there was a design defect. Furthermore, Ned may claim that the fact that the wings came apart was a manufacturing defect. Therefore, because the plane was defective, there was a breach of Wing's duty.

But for the plane being defective, Ned's plane may not have crashed. Further, it is foreseeable that a defective product could result in harm.

It is questionable whether Wings will be liable here.

Strict Products Liability

Ned may also argue that the product was unreasonably dangerous, that a plane that has wings which could come apart when it goes too fast is very dangerous. It is questionable whether Ned will be able to recover here.

Camp Candy v. Shopping Channel

Strict Products Liability

Defined above.

As discussed above, the mosquito lotion will probably not be found to be dangerous; therefore, there was no breach of duty. Shopping Channel will probably not be liable here.

Better Answer

Farmer Fran v. Flyer Ned

Trespass to Land

Trespass to land is the intentional entry upon the land of another without consent or privilege.

When the "runaway" airplane crashed onto Farmer Fran's land, there was an entry upon the land of Farmer Fran without her consent. While Ned may assert that he had no control over the runaway plane and did not intend to intrude on Fran's property, he knew to a substantial degree of certainty that abandoning his plane would eventually result in the plane crashing.

Private Necessity

Ned may assert the defense of private necessity because he jumped from the runaway plane to avoid being seriously injured. This defense will probably work. However, the defense of private necessity is an incomplete defense. Thus, while it will relieve Ned from liability for trespass to land, he will still have to pay for any damages caused.

Therefore, Ned will not be liable for trespass to land.

Conversion

Conversion is the intentional exercise of dominion and control over chattel in possession of another, without consent or privilege.

When Fran's valuable stud bull was killed as a result of the plane crashing into him, Fran was dispossessed of her chattel. Because Ned knew to a substantial degree of certainty that the plane would crash, a court will probably find that Ned had sufficient intent to commit the act that resulted in the conversion. However, Ned could assert the defense of private necessity, and if successful, would not be liable for conversion.

Negligence Per Se

Violation of a statute may prove negligence where (1) the statute was enacted to protect against the type of injury suffered by the plaintiff, (2) the plaintiff was a member of the class the statute was intended to protect, and (3) the defendant has no excuse.

Fran may try to argue that Ned had a duty based on the statute and that his violation of the statute was a breach of that duty. However, Ned will counter that the statute, which set the maximum speed limit for the altitude at which he was flying, was not enacted to protect people like Fran from the loss of their animals.

A court would probably not find Ned negligent on the basis of violating the statute, because the injury suffered by Fran was not the type of harm intended to be prevented by the statute.

Negligence

To recover for negligence, Fran must prove that Ned owed her a *duty*, that he breached that duty, and that Fran suffered injuries, which were actually and proximately caused by Ned's breach.

Duty

Ned had a duty to act as a reasonably prudent flyer or crop duster under the circumstances.

Breach

Fran may argue that Ned breached his duty by spraying the lotion without knowing that it was highly combustible when wet and further, by parachuting from the plane. A court will probably find that his parachuting from the plane was a reasonable thing to do. However, the question of whether Ned knew or should have known that the lotion was highly combustible is a question of fact that will be determined by what was reasonable under the circumstances. It depends on what a reasonable crop duster would do. The court will probably find that he had at least a minimum duty to inquire about the content of the lotion because it was something different than what he normally sprayed. He breached his duty by not doing so.

Actual Cause

Actual cause is determined by the "but for" test. It is true that "but for" Ned spraying the lotion from his plane, Fran's bull would not have been killed.

Proximate Cause

The question of whether Ned's actions were the proximate cause of the death of Fran's bull is determined by whether the injury was a reasonably foreseeable consequence of Ned's actions. Fran would assert that the death of her bull was a foreseeable result of his spraying the lotion from the plane. She would also assert that Ned's action was the direct cause of her damages. However, Ned could argue that the failure of the plane to have any filtering system was an intervening cause. A court will probably find that Ned's actions were a sufficient cause to be held liable, even though the cause may have been an indirect cause.

Damages

Fran may seek to recover general damages for the loss of her bull, and also for any damage to her property. Therefore, Ned will probably be liable for negligence. However, he may be able to seek contribution from Billy.

Strict Liability

Restatement 2nd: One who maintains an abnormally dangerous condition or activity on his premises, or engages in an activity that involves a high risk of harm, may be liable for the harm it causes to other persons or property even though reasonable care has been used to prevent such harm.

Some courts have extended strict liability to crop dusting. Ned's actions here would probably fall under this category. Furthermore, spraying mosquito lotion from a plane is not a matter of common usage, and as the lotion was highly combustible when wet, there was probably a high degree of risk. Therefore, a court may hold Ned strictly liable for the death of Fran's cow, which resulted from his dangerous activity.

Farmer Fran v. Camp Candy (Camp)

Vicarious Liability

Respondeat Superior: A master is vicariously liable for the torts of his servants, which occur within the course and scope of their employment.

Ned owned his own plane. The facts do not indicate that Camp retained any control over Ned's performance. Therefore, a court will probably find Ned to be an independent contractor rather than an employee. Generally, an employer is not vicariously liable for torts committed by independent contractors. However, some courts have found that highly dangerous activities are non-delegable and that one may not escape liability by hiring an independent contractor. Crop dusting is considered by some courts to be a highly dangerous activity.

Therefore, Camp may be liable for harm resulting from such activity. However, if Camp is held vicariously liable, it will be able to bring an action against Flyer Ned for indemnification.

Flyer Ned v. Billy Bongo (Billy)

Negligence

In order to recover for negligence, Ned must prove that Billy owed Ned a duty, that he breached that duty, and that Ned suffered injuries, which were actually and proximately caused by Billy's breach.

Duty

Billy had a duty to act as a reasonably prudent person under the circumstances.

Breach

Ned may assert that Billy breached his duty by providing lotion to Ned, which should not have been used as it was here. A court would probably find that asking someone to spray mosquito lotion from an airplane without making sure it was safe is unreasonable conduct. Therefore, a court will probably find that Billy breached his duty.

Causation

But for Billy asking Ned to spray the lotion from Ned's plane, the plane would not have been damaged. Billy may argue that the defect in the plane was an intervening force. However, the negligence of another will not break the chain of causation. Further, it is foreseeable that asking someone to spray mosquito lotion from a plane without checking whether it would be safe could result in injury to persons or property. Therefore, there is actual and proximate cause.

Damages

Ned may seek to recover general damages for the loss of his plane.

Contributory Negligence

In some jurisdictions, plaintiff's claim for negligence will be barred if defendant can show that plaintiff negligently contributed to his own injury.

Billy will argue that Ned was contributorily negligent in not inquiring into whether the product was safe. Since he was a farmer/crop duster, he would have had more reason to be aware of the possible harm than would Billy. It is questionable whether a court would find Ned to have been contributorily negligent.

Comparative Negligence

In some jurisdictions, the amount plaintiff recovers in damages for negligence will be diminished according to the proportion that the plaintiff's negligence caused his own injury.

If Ned is found to have negligently contributed to his injury in a comparative negligence jurisdiction, he may still be able to recover a portion of his damages.

Assumption of the Risk

Ned did not know that the mosquito lotion was highly combustible when wet; therefore, he did not voluntarily encounter a known risk.

Billy will probably be liable to Ned for the damage to his plane under a negligence theory.

Flyer Ned v. Camp Candy

Vicarious Liability

Respondeat Superior: Defined above.

Billy was the director of Camp. Further, he was trying to further the best interest of the camp by his acts. Therefore, Camp will be liable for Billy's negligence. However, Camp will be able to seek indemnification from Billy.

Flyer Ned v. Shopping Channel (Shopping)

Negligent Products Liability

When a manufacturer of goods places a product into the stream of commerce, it owes a duty to conduct a reasonable inspection of the product and to correct or warn of any dangerous defects, which a reasonable inspection would have revealed.

Breach

Ned may assert that there was a design defect. Because the product contained ethyl zylonene, a substance highly combustible when wet, it could be dangerous, and thus defective. Ned may also assert that his use of the product was foreseeable because Shopping sold the product to them in such a large quantity. However, Ned's arguments will probably fail. The mosquito lotion was not meant to be sprayed from a plane in large quantities. Furthermore, there were no problems with the product in its normal use.

Therefore, a court will probably find that there was no defect, and that Shopping is not liable.

Products—Strict Liability

When a manufacturer or distributor of goods places a product that is defective and unreasonably dangerous into the stream of commerce, it will be held strictly liable for damages resulting from the use of the defective product.

Breach

Ned may assert that the mosquito lotion was unreasonably dangerous because it caused the plane to accelerate above the normal rate. However, Shopping will counter that the product was not dangerous in its normal use. The product was a body lotion and was not designed to be sprayed from airplanes, and Ned misused the product.

Therefore, Ned will probably be unable to prove that the product was dangerous in its normal use. Furthermore, even if he could prove such, Shopping may seek to defend by asserting that Ned assumed the risk by using the product in a different manner than it was intended for. However, to prevail on this argument, Shopping would have to show that Ned knew of the risk.

Shopping will not be liable for strict liability in tort.

Flyer Ned v. Wing and Prayer (Wing)

Products Liability

When a manufacturer or distributor of goods places into the stream of commerce a product that is defective either in design, manufacture, or warning, it may be held liable for injuries resulting from the use of the defective product. There are four different theories of products liability: intentional, negligent, strict liability in tort, and breach of warranty. In order to recover under any of these theories, Ned will have to show that the product was defective.

Ned may argue that the plane was defective in design because the plane was one used for crop dusting and a lack of a filtering system could present an undue risk of harm. Ned may assert that this is evidenced by the fact that 50% of airplane manufacturers install a filtering device. In addition, he may assert that the product did not perform as safely as a reasonable consumer would have expected.

However, Wing may counter that the product was safe in its normal use. It is not a normal use of the plane to spray combustible materials and fly at excess speeds. In addition, there are no facts indicating that the product was unsafe when it was properly used. Finally, Wing may assert that there was no feasible alternative, that is, to put in a filtering system would have greatly increased the cost and such an increase outweighed the risk caused by the lack of a filtering device. A court will probably find that there was not a defect in design because there are no facts indicating that it was unsafe in its normal use.

Ned may further argue that there was a manufacturing defect, because as a result of the increased speed the wings came off. Wing probably did not intend for the wings to come apart when their planes were flown at an increased speed, therefore, a court will probably find there was a manufacturing defect.

Therefore, Ned will probably be able to prove that there was at least a manufacturing defect and will seek to recover under a negligence theory of products liability.

Negligent Products Liability

Duty

Wing as a manufacturer had a duty to make a reasonable inspection of the product and correct or warn of any defects, which a reasonable inspection would reveal.

Breach

Ned may seek to prove breach based on the doctrine of *res ipsa loquitur*. That is, that in the absence of negligence, an airplane's wings do not usually come apart when flown at an increased speed. Furthermore, the product left the manufacturer in a defective condition, thus Wing must have failed to make a reasonable inspection. Otherwise, it would have noticed the defect. Therefore, there was a breach of Wing's duty.

Causation

But for the wings coming off the plane, Ned's plane would not have crashed. In addition, the defect in the plane was the direct cause of Ned's damages. Therefore, there is both actual and proximate cause.

Defenses

Wing may argue that Ned negligently contributed to his injury when he used the plane to spray mosquito lotion over a twenty-five-mile radius, and that such an action was a misuse of the product.

However, Ned could counter that the plane was meant to spray other substances and therefore, that his use was foreseeable. Wing's defense of contributory negligence will probably fail.

Therefore, Wing will be liable for the damages.

Products—Breach of Warranty

Ned may also assert that there was a breach of the implied warranty of merchantability, because the plane, by not having any filtering system, was not fit for ordinary use. However, Wing will counter that spraying mosquito lotion is not a normal use of the plane, but rather was a misuse of the product. Wing will probably prevail in this argument and therefore, will not be liable for breach of implied warranty.

Camp Candy v. Shopping Channel

Strict Product Liability

Defined above.

If Camp tries to bring an action against Shopping for strict products liability, it will probably fail. As discussed above, the product was not dangerous in its normal use. Further, while Camp may claim that Shopping should have foreseen an unusual use of the product by selling such a large quantity and should have warned Camp, this argument will probably fail.

The product, if used properly, was not unreasonably dangerous, nor is it likely that a court would find Camp's use as reasonably foreseeable. Therefore, Shopping will probably not be liable.

Statute of Limitations

The facts indicate that Billy first purchased the mosquito lotion three years ago and it appears as though the series of events resulting in the above actions occurred not long thereafter. Depending on what the applicable statute of limitations is and how long ago the above events occurred, it is possible that the parties may be barred from bringing suit.

What Makes the Second Answer Better?

The main reason that the second answer is better is because it includes more of the issues. Issue spotting is a big part of a torts exam, unlike a contracts exam, which involves much more analysis. Very often students do well on a torts exam as long as they address most of the issues, even if they do not discuss them in great depth. The reason for this is that there is usually only one hour in which to complete the essay and only so many points possible for each issue. The more issues you spot and discuss, the more points you will earn. If you fail to raise some issues because you spent too much time discussing other issues, your score will suffer.

In addition to covering more issues, the second essay has a more complete discussion on the major issues. Through practice and a thorough understanding of the law, you will be able to discern which issues deserve more time. The second answer includes more analysis of those issues that are more complex and important.

In conclusion, the key is not only to cover as many issues as possible, but also to distinguish the major issues from the minor ones. Allocation of time is important so that your essay answer includes short but complete discussions of the minor issues, and a full analysis of the major issues.

CONTRACTS

Final Exam Essay Question

Ag, an agricultural chemical company that develops, manufactures, and markets herbicides and pesticides, needed to install new production equipment to produce ZapEm, a granulated substance that kills bugs on contact. The process requires a high-powered dryer that will take wet chemicals and quickly dry them into granulated form.

On February 1, Ag contacted Dry, a manufacturer of drying equipment and requested information and a price quote for one of its Class A dryers. Dry faxed information to Ag, along with a standard purchase agreement with $500,000 filled in as the price. By the agreement, Dry agreed to install the dryer and train the purchaser's employees on how to operate the dryer.

The president of Ag signed the agreement and faxed it back, but added the following language at the end of the agreement:

> Purchase being made upon the condition that Dry completes its development of ECO, an energy efficient heating system, and includes the ECO technology in the dryer delivered to Ag. Time is of the essence. The dryer must be installed and operating by November 1, or we will lose about $5,000 per day in profits.

Ag estimated that its profits would be this high because of the anticipated demand for ZapEm in the spring of the following year. Dry faxed a note back to Ag saying that manufacturing of the dryer had begun and that it would be operating before November 1.

Dry completed development of the ECO technology and utilized it in the dryer, which it then installed at Ag's facility. Dry also satisfactorily trained Ag's employees in the use of the dryer, but when the dryer was tested on October 31, the ECO technology did not function properly.

Dry dismantled a portion of the dryer and took it back to its factory for repairs. Dry employees said that they would have the dryer running again within a few days. After seven days, Ag called Dry and inquired about the repairs. Dry said it needed a few more days. Ag said that if the repairs were not made within five days, it would revoke its acceptance. Six days later, Ag had not heard from Dry. Ag then contracted with WorksRight to supply an equivalent dryer, utilizing ENVIRO technology, for $750,000, and faxed Dry notice of its revocation of acceptance.

As WorksRight was completing installation on December 1, Dry attempted to deliver the replacement parts for its dryer. Ag refused the parts and sued for damages. Dry, in turn, sued for the full purchase price.

Discuss the claims and defenses of each party and the likely results of the litigation.

Good Answer

UCC v. Common Law

The UCC covers all contracts for the sale of goods defined as all items identifiable and movable at the time of formation.

The contract in question involves the sale of a dryer, which is considered "goods." Therefore, the UCC applies.

Merchants

As Dry is a manufacturer of dryers, it will be found to be a merchant. Ag's work required use of the kind of dryer involved here, thus it is arguable that Ag had knowledge or skill related to the dryer. Therefore, it would also be considered a merchant. As merchants, both parties will be held to a higher standard of good faith.

Offer

An offer is an outward manifestation of present contractual intent, which is definite in terms, and which is communicated in such a way as to create in the offeree a reasonable expectation that the offeror is willing to enter into a contract.

Ag inquired into the price of one of Dry's Class A dryers by requesting information and a price quote. In response, Dry faxed Ag a standard purchase agreement with the purchase price filled in. It is likely that a court would find that Dry made an offer for: One dryer at the price of $500,000 to be sold by Dry to Ag. At Common Law, this offer would fail for lack of definiteness because it omits a time for performance. However, this contract falls under the UCC, which allows a contract to be made in any manner sufficient to show agreement. Here the most important element is present—the quantity. The other elements not included could be completed by what is reasonable. Therefore, there is a valid offer.

Acceptance

An acceptance is an outward manifestation of unequivocal assent to the terms of the offer.

The president of Ag signed the agreement and faxed it back. However, he also added terms to the contract, that is, he added the condition that ECO technology be developed and used in the dryer and also a "time is of the essence" clause. Generally, between merchants an acceptance is valid even if it contains additional terms unless acceptance is expressly conditioned upon acceptance of the added terms.

Because Ag's fax stated: "Purchase being made upon the condition that . . ." it may be argued that the acceptance was conditioned upon those terms becoming part of the contract. If this were the case, then Ag's fax would not be considered an acceptance. However, even if this were true, Dry responded with another fax stating that the manufacturing of the dryer had begun and that it would be operating by November 1, indicating that it consented to the additional terms. Therefore, a court would find a valid acceptance.

UCC 2-207—Additional and Different Terms

Between merchants, such additional terms will become a part of the contract unless: (1) the offer expressly limits acceptance on its own terms; (2) the additional terms would materially alter the offer; (3) within a reasonable time period, the offeror notifies the offeree that he objects to the additional terms.

It is arguable that the added "time is of the essence clause" and the condition that ECO technology be used materially altered the offer, thus preventing an acceptance. However, Dry responded to the fax with the additional terms with a note saying it had begun manufacturing the dryer and that performance would be done before November 1.

Therefore, there was an acceptance of even the additional terms. Furthermore, a court would most likely find the contract to include those additional terms based on the actions of the parties.

Consideration

That which is bargained for and given in exchange requiring both mutual benefit and mutual detriment.

Ag was bargaining for a dryer in exchange for payment, and Dry was bargaining for payment in return for one of its dryers.

Therefore, there is valid consideration.

Statute of Frauds

Contracts for the sale of goods of $500 or more fall within the Statute of Frauds and are required to be in writing to be enforceable.

The contract in question involved the sale of a dryer at $500,000. Therefore, it falls within the Statute of Frauds and is required to be in writing. The contract in question consisted of a series of faxes between Ag and Dry. The agreement was signed by Ag and faxed back to Dry. Because all the requisite terms are present, it is enforceable against Ag. If Dry had signed the faxed agreement before the fax, or if Dry signed the note faxed back to Ag, the court will find the agreement enforceable against Dry.

Therefore, a court will probably find that the agreement or the combination of faxed communications will constitute an agreement that satisfies the Statute of Frauds.

Ag v. Dry

Breach

A breach is an unjustified failure to perform a contractual duty.

Dry did not meet the deadline to have the dryer in place and failed to deliver conforming goods. In addition to this, even if a court were to find that the deadline was waived when Ag allowed Dry to repair the parts, it would probably find that Dry still breached by failing to perform within a reasonable time. In addition, after waiting a few days for the dryer to be repaired and not getting a response, then setting a deadline and hearing nothing from Dry, it is arguable that Ag demanded at least adequate assurances and that Dry failed to give such assurances. Therefore, a court will probably find that Dry breached its duty under the contract. In addition, this will probably be found to be a major breach because it goes to the essence of the contract.

Remedies

Ag as the purchaser has a duty to mitigate its damages under the contract. In this case, his duty would be to "cover" and buy a substitute product. Ag will be able to recover the difference between the contract price and the cover price.

Consequential Damages—Hadley v. Baxendale

Compensation will be given for those consequential damages, which the defendant at the time the contract was made had reason to foresee as a probable result of his breach.

Ag will also seek to recover the $5,000 a day in profits that it lost as a result of the dryer not being finished on time. As a result of Dry's failure to deliver the dryer in working order on time, Ag was forced to wait several days, waiting for Dry to repair the dryer. In addition, Ag did not finish repairing the dryer even after two weeks of waiting and as a result Dry purchased one from another company in an effort to mitigate his damages. Ag ended up not receiving a working dryer until one month later.

The $5,000-a-day loss in profits was stated in the additional terms, therefore, it was foreseeable by Dry as a result of his breach. Therefore, Ag will probably be able to recover consequential damages for the profits he lost as a result of not having a dryer for those days.

Avoidable Consequences Rule

The plaintiff cannot recover for damages that he could have reasonably avoided.

Ag had a duty to mitigate his damages. The facts indicate that once Ag realized that Dry would not perform, he contacted WorksRight to supply an equivalent dryer. There are no facts to show that Ag had any other options. Therefore, it appears as though Ag did all that he could to mitigate his damages and will be able to recover not only for his actual losses, but also for any incidental damages incurred as a result of his efforts to mitigate his damages.

Dry v. Ag

Dry would like to recover for the price of the dryer under the contract. In order to do so, Dry must show that it performed under the contract, thus giving rise to Ag's duty to pay.

Conditions

A condition is an act or event not certain to occur, which unless excused gives rise to or extinguishes a duty to tender performance under the terms of a contract.

Constructive Condition Precedent

A longer performance is a constructive condition precedent to a shorter performance.

Ag will assert that manufacturing the dryer is the longer performance and is a constructive condition precedent to Ag's duty to pay.

Express Condition—Time Is of the Essence Clause

Ag may also assert that the "time is of the essence" clause is an express condition precedent to his duty to pay. The language used made it clear that the clause was a condition in that Ag stated that the purchase was being made "upon condition that." Furthermore, "time is of the essence" clauses are usually found to be expressed conditions. Therefore, a court will probably find that Ag's duty to perform, that is, tender payment, was expressly conditioned upon Dry's duty to manufacture and install the dryer.

Satisfaction of Conditions

Dry may argue that it satisfied the condition by installing the dryer by November 1 and by developing the ECO technology. However, the dryer did not actually function properly by November 1, rather, Dry took a portion of the dryer back to its factory for repairs and was not done repairing it by the required date. Therefore, there was no satisfaction of either condition.

Dry may also seek to show that their condition to perform first was excused by waiver.

Waiver

A waiver occurs where a party proceeds with his performance and ignores the nonoccurrence of a condition by the other party.

Dry may argue that when Ag did not say anything about the dryer not working, but rather inquired about the repairs, Ag waived the condition precedent. Dry may also claim that Ag accepted the nonconforming goods by not immediately rejecting them when they did not work. Ag would say that it did not waive the condition and that it had not accepted the goods. Even if it did accept the goods, Ag has the right to revoke its acceptance under the UCC. Therefore, it is unlikely that a court would find that Ag waived complete performance of the condition and it is likely that Dry still had a duty to satisfy the condition, at least within a few days.

Breach

If the court found that there was an effective waiver of the condition, Dry's recovery would depend on whether Ag accepted the goods, or whether it wrongfully revoked its acceptance. If Ag accepted, or if it wrongfully revoked, Dry would be able to recover for Ag's refusal to pay the contract.

A buyer has a right to inspect the goods prior to payment or acceptance of the goods. Ag would claim that it inspected the goods in the process of installation and testing, but claim that it never accepted the dryer because it did not work. Even if it was considered to have accepted the dryer, Ag took the proper steps to revoke the acceptance when the problem was not solved.

Dry may say that by allowing the dryer to remain there and by allowing Dry to attempt repairs there was an acceptance, or that the revocation was not justifiable. Dry's argument will probably fail because Ag gave Dry notice of its intent to revoke and only allowed the dryer to stay there in the belief that the defect would be cured. After Ag gave Dry notice that it would revoke its acceptance in five days and Dry did not respond, there was a justifiable revocation of acceptance.

Therefore, Ag had no duty to pay because it gave an effective and timely revocation of his acceptance. However, Ag will have to return the dryer to Dry.

Remedies

If the court were to find that the revocation was not effective or not justifiable, Dry would be able to recover the difference between the contract price and the price for which Dry is able to sell the dryer, pursuant to its duty to mitigate damages.

Better Answer

UCC v. Common Law

This contract involves the sale of a dryer, which is considered "goods" as defined in the UCC. Goods are tangible, personal property that are movable and identifiable at the time of the contract. However, the contract also called for its installation, and instruction on how to operate the dryer. Thus, the contract covers a combination of both goods and services. Where this is the case, there are several tests used to determine whether the UCC is applicable.

Predominant Factor Test

The total cost of the dryer under the contract was $500,000. The facts do not indicate how much was for the dryer and how much was for the installation and the training. It is likely that the majority of the price was for the dryer, based on the fact that Ag had asked for a price quote on the dryer and not for installation and training. It is apparent that the dryer was the predominant factor.

Gravamen of the Injury Test

Under this test, the court looks to see what was the nature of the injury. Ag's employees received the training and the product was installed. However, the dryer failed to work properly. Therefore, the injury went to the actual product, that is, the dryer. Thus, under this test the UCC would govern.

Therefore, under either test the contract will be governed by the UCC.

Merchants

A merchant is one who regularly deals with the particular type of goods involved in the transaction or otherwise holds himself out as having knowledge or skill peculiar to the type of goods involved.

Dry is a merchant because it deals in goods of the kind that are the subject of this contract and it has specialized knowledge about dryers. In addition, while Ag was an agricultural chemical company, one can assume that it had at least some specialized knowledge of the type of dryer involved in the transaction.

Therefore, a court will certainly find that Dry is a merchant and it will probably find that Ag is also. As a result, both parties will be held to the standard of honesty in fact and the observance of reasonable commercial standards.

Offer

An offer is an outward manifestation of present contractual intent, which is definite in terms, and which is communicated in such a way as to create in the offeree a reasonable expectation that the offeror is willing to enter into a contract.

When Ag contacted Dry requesting information and a price quote on one of its Class A dryers, there was no present intent to contract on the part of Ag. Rather, Ag was merely making an inquiry.

When Dry responded to Ag's request by faxing a standard purchase agreement with the purchase price filled in, it was an offer based on the following terms: Quantity—One; Time for Performance—Not mentioned; Identity of the Parties—Ag and Dry; Price—$500,000; Subject Matter—Dryer.

Under the Common Law, all terms had to be present in order to have a valid offer. However, under the UCC, a contract for the sale of goods may be made in any manner sufficient to show agreement, including conduct of the parties that recognize the existence of such a contract. Even though one or more terms are left open, a contract for the sale of goods does not fail for indefiniteness if the parties have intended a contract. To satisfy the Statute of Frauds requirement of the UCC, a contract for the sale of goods of $500 or more must be in writing and must at least include the quantity.

Therefore, when Dry faxed the purchase order to Ag, there was a valid offer.

Acceptance

An acceptance is an outward manifestation of unequivocal assent to the terms of the offer.

When the president of Ag signed the agreement and faxed it back with the additional language, an acceptance was made. The issue is what effect, if any, did the additional language have on the acceptance.

Under the UCC, even if an acceptance states terms additional to or different from those offered, it operates as an acceptance unless acceptance is expressly made conditional on assent to the additional or different terms. When the president of Ag signed the agreement and faxed it back, it included added language regarding a "time is of the essence" clause and the condition that ECO technology be developed and used. Dry may argue that the additional language was an acceptance that was conditioned upon its assent. But even if it was, Dry effectively gave its consent by its fax saying that production began and that the dryer would be operational by November 1.

Therefore, there was a valid acceptance.

UCC 2-207—Additional and Different Terms

Between merchants, additional terms in an acceptance will become a part of the contract unless: (1) the original offer expressly limits acceptance on its own terms; (2) the additional terms would materially alter the contract; (3) within a reasonable time period, the offeror notifies the offeree that he objects to the additional terms.

While it could be argued by either party that the additional terms were a material alteration, the terms would probably still become a part of the contract because of the parties' subsequent actions. Dry responded to the fax with the additional terms with a note saying it had begun manufacturing the dryer and that performance would be done before November 1.

Therefore, there was a valid acceptance. Furthermore, a court will likely find the contract to include the additional terms based on the actions of the parties.

Consideration

Consideration is the bargained-for exchange of something of legal value between the parties. It is what induces the parties to act and it usually requires mutual benefit and mutual detriment.

Ag was bargaining for a dryer in exchange for payment of $500,000, and Dry was bargaining for payment in return for one of its dryers.

Therefore, there is valid consideration.

Statute of Frauds

When there is a contract for the sale of goods for $500 or more, the agreement must be in writing to be enforceable under the Statute of Frauds. The writing may be incomplete as long as it indicates that an agreement has been made and that it was signed by the party to be charged. In this situation, Ag and Dry are both defendants because each has a claim against the other.

The contract in this question was for the sale of a dryer at $500,000; therefore, the contract falls within the Statute of Frauds. In this case, the contract consisted of a series of faxes. We do not know if the president of Dry signed the agreement before faxing it to Ag. If so, the Statute would have been satisfied with respect to both parties because Ag signed the agreement. If not, it was probably faxed with a cover sheet that included the company name etc., and Ag would claim that a signed cover sheet would be sufficient to bind Dry.

The writings that exist satisfy the Statute of Frauds and the writing is enforceable against both parties. The parties could also assert that part performance takes the contract out of the Statute of Frauds, at least to the degree of performance.

Ag v. Dry

Breach

A breach is an unjustified failure to perform a contractual duty.

Ag will have a claim for breach of contract against Dry because it delivered nonconforming goods and because it did not supply an operating dryer by November 1. Ag will claim that Dry's breach was a major breach because it went to the essence of the contract.

Dry will defend itself by claiming that Ag "waived" the time deadline (discussed below) and that Ag did not give Dry a reasonable time to cure the nonconformity.

Under the UCC, whether there is a breach of a contract for the sale of goods depends upon whether the goods supplied were conforming and whether the Buyer accepted those goods.

2-513 provides that a Buyer has a right to inspection before payment or acceptance of goods. Ag would claim that it had not accepted the goods because the dryer was not yet functioning. Dry would argue that Ag accepted the goods because on October 31 the dryer was in place and Ag's employees had been trained.

A court could justifiably rule that Ag had not yet accepted the goods, but because Ag had allowed the dryer to be installed, a court might rule that there was an acceptance. But even if the court ruled that there was an acceptance, Ag has a right to revoke its acceptance pursuant to 2-608.

This section provides that a Buyer may revoke his acceptance when the nonconformity substantially impairs its value to him, and if he has accepted the product on the reasonable assumption that its nonconformity would be cured, and it has not been seasonably cured. Such revocation must occur within a reasonable time. The revocation is not effective until the Buyer notifies the Seller, and once the revocation is properly done, the Buyer has the same rights as if he rejected the goods. Therefore, whether Ag rejected the goods or revoked its acceptance, it is in the same position to make a claim against Dry for breach.

The dryer that Dry installed did not work, so it was nonconforming. Ag would say that it only allowed the dryer to remain in place upon the reasonable assumption that the problem would be cured. The assumption was reasonable because Dry said it would only take a few days to fix it. When the nonconformity was not cured within a reasonable time, Ag had the right to revoke its acceptance, if there had been one.

Ag then gave notice to Dry of its intent to revoke if the repairs were not made within five days, but Dry did not respond. After five days, Ag faxed a notice of revocation to Dry. Dry did not return with the replacement parts until over fifteen days after the revocation.

Dry may argue that the revocation was not within a reasonable time, but under the circumstances, a court would probably find that the revocation was within a reasonable time. It was only twelve or thirteen days after the performance date of November 1.

Ag has a solid claim for breach of contract.

Remedies

Because Ag's revocation was reasonable and it properly notified Dry, Ag would have the rights under 2-711 and 2-712 to "cover" and buy a substitute product. The Common Law avoidable consequences rule and duty to mitigate is incorporated into the UCC under the requirement to act in good faith. Between merchants, this not only means honesty in fact but also following reasonable commercial standards. 2-712 requires a Buyer when it "covers" to make in good faith and without unreasonable delay any reasonable purchase of goods in substitution for those due from the Seller. Ag did this.

Therefore, Ag has a right to recover from Dry the difference between the contract price and the cover price. This would put Ag in the same position had the contract been completed.

Ag could also claim incidental and consequential damages as a result of Dry not fulfilling its promise to have the dryer operational by November 1. Consequential damages are permitted under 2-712 (cover) and 2-715, which is comparable to the doctrine of *Hadley v. Baxendale* with respect to Common Law contracts.

2-715 defines incidental damages as those resulting from the Seller's breach, including costs of inspection, transportation, care, and custody of goods rightfully rejected, and other reasonable expenses incident to the breach.

Consequential damages are any losses resulting from general or particular requirements or needs of which the Seller at the time of contracting had reason to know and which could not reasonably be prevented by cover or otherwise.

In this case, Dry knew that Ag would lose about $5,000 per day after November 1. So, Ag can recover incidental damages, including those associated with cover, the difference between the contract price and the cover price ($250,000) plus consequential damages, such as lost profits.

Dry v. Ag

Dry will claim that Ag breached the contract and that it should be paid the contract price. In order to succeed, Dry would have to prove that it satisfied all the conditions that were in the contract, or that the conditions were excused.

Conditions

A condition is an act or event not certain to occur, which unless satisfied or excused gives rise to or extinguishes a duty to tender performance under the terms of a contract. A plaintiff must demonstrate that all the conditions that it was required to satisfy were either satisfied or excused before the defendant has a duty to perform.

Ag had no conditions to satisfy before Dry had a duty to perform, but Dry did have conditions that needed to be satisfied before Ag had a duty to pay.

Express Conditions

Express conditions are expressly agreed to in the contract. They require complete performance to be satisfied.

Assuming that the additional terms are included in the contract, the purchase was conditioned upon Dry developing and incorporating into the dryer the ECO technology. Dry did develop the technology and utilized it in the Class A dryer delivered to Ag and therefore satisfied this condition.

Time Is of the Essence Clause

The requirement that the dryer be operating before November 1 was also an express condition. Time is of the essence clauses are express conditions that must be completely satisfied or excused.

While Dry might argue that the requirement that the dryer be operating is only a promise rather than a condition, the condition seems to include both the time and operation element. Therefore, Ag's duty to perform, that is, tender payment, was expressly conditioned upon Dry's duty to manufacture and install the dryer.

Satisfaction of Condition

Dry may argue that it satisfied the condition because the dryer was installed by November 1. However, the dryer was not operating by November 1. Dry took a portion of the dryer back to its factory for repairs and was not done repairing it by the required date. Therefore, Dry failed to satisfy its condition.

Dry may also seek to show that their condition to perform first was excused.

Waiver

A waiver occurs where a party proceeds with his performance and ignores the nonoccurrence of a condition by the other party.

Dry would argue that when Ag did not say anything about the dryer not working, but rather inquired about the repairs, it waived performance of the condition at least as to the express condition. In addition, Dry would say that Ag accepted the nonconforming goods by not immediately rejecting them when they did not work.

If the court rules that there was no waiver, Dry may not recover. If the court rules that there was a waiver, Dry would be subject to the rights of Ag governed by the UCC with respect to acceptance of goods or the revocation of acceptance (discussed above).

Also, Ag could show that it retracted any apparent waiver.

Retraction

A waiver may be retracted if neither party has detrimentally relied upon the waiver.

After waiting seven days for Dry to repair the parts, Ag called Dry to inquire about the repairs. In response, Dry stated that it needed a few more days, to which Ag stated, "if the repairs were not made in five days it would revoke its acceptance." Ag may assert that this was a retraction of its waiver. The facts do not indicate whether Dry relied to his detriment upon the waiver. Furthermore, Ag did not hear from Dry after six days and did not receive performance until several weeks later. A court could reasonably find that there was a valid retraction.

Breach and Remedies

A breach is an unjustified failure to perform a contractual duty.

Unless Dry can prove that it satisfied its conditions, or that its conditions were excused by waiver, Ag had no duty to pay.

But even if there was a waiver, the rights of Ag and Dry are governed by the UCC and Dry would only have a right to recover from Ag if Dry can prove that Ag wrongfully revoked its acceptance. This is unlikely for the reasons discussed under the Ag v. Dry.

But if the revocation was wrongful, Dry would have the remedies provided by 2-708. Dry will be able to recover the difference between the contract price and the amount for which Dry is able to sell the dryer, plus incidental damages. If the difference between the resale price and the contract price does not put Dry in as good a position as performance would have, then the measure of damages is the profit Dry would have had from full performance (2-708).

But if the revocation was rightful, which is the best conclusion, Dry would not be able to recover anything from Ag. However, Ag will have to return the dryer to Dry.

What Makes the Second Answer Better?

After reading the answers to the contracts essay question, you should readily see the major differences between torts and contracts. The nature of the questions and the type of analysis used in answering the questions are different. Torts questions involved many separate claims that should be analyzed separately. In contracts, the issues build upon one another and, depending on your conclusion on one issue, you proceed to address the next issue in a consistent way. For this reason, more time is needed to organize and outline the answer to a contracts question. One needs to "think down the road" about what implications the answer to one issue has on other issues.

There are several noticeable differences between the two answers. The second answer flows logically with each element building upon the last. It also includes a much more complete and in-depth analysis of each of the issues. For example, while the first answer rightly concludes that the UCC applies, it fails to discuss the various tests used to determine if the UCC controls. Because time is always limited in an examination, you will need to decide how thoroughly you discuss each issue. As you outline your answer, you will see which issues are most important and you should allocate your time accordingly. In this particular question, the application of the UCC was clear and if the discussion had been somewhat shorter, full credit would still have been given. The detailed discussion in the "Better Answer" was given to illustrate the mental analysis one must go through, not necessarily to illustrate what one should have written down.

Other issues, like whether Dry satisfied the conditions and what UCC provisions applied to determine the remedies available, required more discussion. These issues were major ones that had credible support for each side. While the good answer discusses many of the general rules, the second answer states the applicable UCC rules and is much more precise. Also, you can see that the IRAC analysis was more complete and that the adversarial method was used when appropriate.

CRIMINAL LAW

Final Exam Essay Question

Jerry and Bill drove from Kansas City to Oklahoma City for a car convention. They arrived at 9 p.m. and immediately drove to the "Sleepy Inn Hotel" and went to bed. At approximately 11:00 p.m., Jill and John snuck into Jerry and Bill's room and tried to steal Jerry's watch. Bill, hearing their footsteps, turned on his tabletop light. This startled Jill and John, who ran for the door. Jill grabbed the keys to Jerry's new car as they exited the hotel room.

Making their way into the parking lot, Jill and John then drove to Bob's All-Night Car Sales and sold Jerry's new car for $2,500 cash. Bob in turn sold the car to Jimmy for $3,500. Jimmy is an undercover agent for the Oklahoma Department of Revenue. Jimmy earlier had told Bob that he would buy as many stolen sports cars as Bob could "get his hands on."

Jimmy, in turn, offered the car to George, who politely turned him down. Jimmy then spent over five hours trying to convince Rachel to purchase the car for $4,000. Jimmy never indicated to Rachel that the car was stolen. Rachel, although hesitant, said she would have to wait until next week, when she would turn eighteen, to get the money from her savings account. After one week, Rachel, still reluctant, nevertheless paid Jimmy. Jimmy promptly arrested Rachel.

Meanwhile, across town, Jerry and Bill had just arrived at the convention center by taxi. There they met Jill and John, who had been drinking heavily all afternoon. Much to Jill's shock, John pulled out a gun and took Jerry's watch and billfold. Jill and John ran to an alleyway four blocks from the convention center, where Jill took the checkbook from John and wrote out four checks, signed Jerry's name, and cashed the checks at four different grocery stores in Oklahoma City. John, fed up with Jill, said that he was not going to have anything to do with a "bad-check artist" and left for Tulsa. Later the next day, Jill turned herself in to the local police, stating that she had but one rule, "I have never and will never have anything to do with guns."

Please fully discuss all of the crimes addressed by the fact pattern and explain the potential outcome for all defendants at trial. Please discuss all of the crimes in the order of their occurrence. Failure to do so will result in a reduction of points.

Good Answer

State v. John and Jill

Common Law Burglary

Common Law burglary is the breaking and entering of the dwelling of another, in the nighttime, with specific intent to commit a felony therein.

John and Jill broke into Jerry and Bill's room late at night. It is reasonable to conclude that they intended to commit a larceny because upon entering the room, they tried to steal a watch and stole the keys to Jerry's new car. Larceny is a felony under Common Law. The state will assert that the hotel room was a dwelling because Jerry and Bill were sleeping there.

If the state is successful on the dwelling issue, John and Jill will be guilty of Common Law burglary.

Modern Law Burglary

Modern law defines burglary as the trespassory entering of any structure, with intent to commit a crime therein.

The intent to commit a crime is shown by John and Jill's actions. A hotel room is certainly a structure, and the entering was trespassory. Therefore, John and Jill will be found guilty of modern law burglary.

Attempted Larceny

An attempt is the substantial step toward perpetration of an intended crime (larceny). Larceny is the trespassory taking and carrying away of the property of another, with the specific intent to permanently deprive.

The facts indicate that the defendants broke into Jerry and Bill's room and tried to steal Jerry's watch but were unsuccessful. Thus, they entered the zone of perpetration, and were physically proximate to the scene of the attempted crime. Therefore, they will be guilty of attempted larceny.

Larceny of Keys and Car

Larceny is the trespassory taking and carrying away of the property of another, with the specific intent to permanently deprive.

Here, Jill grabbed the keys to Jerry's new car on her way out of the room, and together she and John drove off in the car. This constituted a taking and carrying away. Their later action of selling the car to a third party is evidence of a clear intent never to return it to Jerry.

Thus, a larceny was committed.

Modern Law Burglary of Car

Modern law burglary is the trespassory entering of any structure with the intent to commit a crime therein.

Under modern law definitions, a car is also considered a structure. When John and Jill entered the car without permission, it was a trespassory entering. Since their purpose in entry was to steal the car (a crime), they committed modern law burglary of the car.

State v. John

Robbery

Robbery is the trespassory taking of another's personal property from his person or presence by violence or intimidation.

When John pulled out a gun and took Jerry's watch and billfold, a robbery occurred because the taking was from Jerry's person and by force. Furthermore, it can be assumed that John intended to permanently deprive Jerry of his property.

Therefore, John is guilty of robbery.

State v. Bob

After stealing the car, John and Jill took it to Bob's All-Night Car Sales, and sold it to Bob for $2,500.

Receiving Stolen Property

This crime occurs when there is a receipt of stolen property, knowing it is stolen, with intent to deprive the owner thereof.

Knowledge of the stolen nature of the car can be inferred from the circumstances. Here, Bob should have known the car was stolen because it was brought to him late at night, and people rarely sell brand new cars for the low price of $2,500. Furthermore, Bob had already entered a deal to sell stolen cars to Jimmy, so he had requisite knowledge. He also actually received the car, and had the intent to deprive the owners by selling the car to a third party. Thus, he is guilty of receiving stolen property.

Conspiracy to Sell Stolen Cars

Conspiracy is an agreement between two or more persons to commit an illegal act (in this case selling stolen cars). There must be: (1) an intent to agree, (2) an actual agreement, and (3) under modern rules, an overt act in furtherance of the conspiracy.

Jimmy had told Bob he would buy as many stolen cars as he could get his hands on. Bob sold the stolen car to him, thus evidencing his agreement to buy and sell stolen cars. Furthermore, the selling of the car to Jimmy was an overt act in furtherance of this agreement. However, Bob will argue that there was no agreement because Jimmy was an undercover agent and had no actual intent to buy and sell stolen cars. Therefore, there was no agreement.

While Bob cannot be convicted under Common Law rules, the Model Penal Code provides for a unilateral conspiracy whereby a conspiracy exists as long as there is an agreement by the defendant.

Entrapment

A defendant is allowed to claim the defense of entrapment if he was induced by a police officer or other law enforcement agent to commit the crime. This defense is available for non-serious crimes where law enforcement officers entrapped the defendant. Under the traditional view, entrapment is not a defense if the defendant was already predisposed to commit the crime—the officer must create the intent to commit the crime. Under the modern objective view, courts look at the conduct of the law enforcement officer and find entrapment when the crime was committed in response to law enforcement activity, which would be likely to cause a reasonable person to commit a crime.

While Bob may claim that Jimmy entrapped him by pretending to be interested in buying stolen cars, the state will show that (1) Bob was already predisposed to sell stolen cars, and (2) Jimmy did not engage in conduct which would entice a reasonable person to commit a crime.

Entrapment will not be a successful defense.

State v. Rachel

Receiving Stolen Property

Defined above.

The state may assert that Rachel received stolen property when she bought the car from Jimmy, the undercover officer. Rachel should have known that the car was stolen based upon the fact that it was being sold for $4,000. In addition, by purchasing the car, Rachel intended to deprive the owner of his property. However, Rachel will assert that she was never told that the car was stolen. In addition to this, she may assert that when she bought the car it was not stolen property because it had been recovered by law enforcement (Jimmy was an undercover agent.) Furthermore, if these arguments fail, Rachel may assert the defense of entrapment.

Entrapment

Defined above.

Rachel was not already predisposed to purchase the car. On the contrary, it took Jimmy over five hours to convince her to buy the car, and even then she was reluctant. Therefore, even if the state finds that the elements for receiving stolen property are met, Rachel will be able to assert successfully the defense of entrapment.

Therefore, Rachel will probably not be found guilty of receiving stolen property.

State v. Jill

Forgery

Forgery is the fraudulent making or altering of a writing of apparent legal significance with intent to defraud another.

Jill forged Jerry's name on four checks with intent to defraud him by cashing them.

Voluntary Intoxication

While voluntary intoxication is not really a defense in and of itself, it may be used to show that the defendant did not have the necessary specific intent. Jill had been drinking heavily all afternoon. In addition, forgery is a specific intent crime. Thus, she may argue that as a result of her intoxication she was unable to form the requisite intent needed for a conviction of forgery. However, there are no facts indicating that her intoxication prevented her from having the specific intent here. Therefore, this defense will probably fail.

Therefore, Jill will be found guilty of forgery.

Uttering

Uttering is offering as genuine an instrument known to be false, with intent to defraud.

Jill cashed the four checks (offered them as genuine) at four grocery stores around town with the intent to defraud Jerry of his money. Uttering is a specific intent crime. Therefore, Jill may also seek to assert that due to her voluntary intoxication, she did not have the requisite intent. However, as previously discussed, this defense will probably fail. Therefore, she will be found guilty of uttering.

Better Answer

State v. John and Jill

Conspiracy to Commit Burglary

A conspiracy is the agreement between two or more persons to commit an illegal act. There must be (1) an intent to agree, (2) actual agreement, and (3) under modern rules, an overt act in furtherance of the conspiracy.

Here, the facts show that John and Jill snuck into Jerry and Bill's hotel room to steal Jerry's watch. Although an express agreement is not specifically mentioned, it can be inferred from these facts that John and Jill intended to agree and actually agreed to commit the crime of stealing Jerry's watch before committing the crime. In addition, the act of breaking into the room was an overt act.

Therefore, they can be convicted of conspiracy.

Vicarious Liability—Pinkerton's Rule

Pinkerton's Rule states that each member of a conspiracy is liable for crimes committed by all other members as long as the crimes were a reasonably foreseeable result of the conspiracy and done in furtherance of it.

Since John and Jill are joint members of a conspiracy, they will be guilty of all the crimes committed, which were a foreseeable result of their conspiracy, even if the other member is actually the one who physically committed them. These include: the attempted larceny of the watch, the larceny of the keys and car, and the burglary of the car.

Common Law Burglary

Common Law burglary is the breaking and entering of the dwelling of another, in the nighttime, with specific intent to commit a felony therein.

Here, the defendants broke into and entered an occupied hotel room at 11:00 p.m. with intent to commit a larceny. Thus we see that all the elements are met, with the possible exception of dwelling. Defendants will argue that a hotel room is not a permanent dwelling where people live, but is actually a business. State will argue that a dwelling is a place used for sleep, and that at the time of the breaking, individuals were sleeping in the hotel room. The state will likely win.

Therefore, defendants should be guilty of Common Law burglary.

Modern Law Burglary

Modern law defines burglary as the trespassory entering of any structure, with intent to commit a crime therein.

As discussed above, a court will probably find that there was a Common Law burglary. However, if the court finds the hotel room was not a dwelling, it was at least a structure. Therefore, the defendants will be guilty of modern law burglary.

Attempted Larceny

An attempt is the substantial step toward perpetration of an intended crime (larceny). Larceny is the trespassory taking and carrying away of the property of another, with the specific intent to permanently deprive. Here, it says the defendants snuck into the room and tried to steal Jerry's watch. Thus, they had entered the zone of perpetration, and were physically proximate to the scene of the intended crime. There was an attempted larceny of the watch.

Larceny of Keys and Car

Larceny is the trespassory taking and carrying away of the property of another, with specific intent to permanently deprive.

Here, Jill grabbed the keys to Jerry's new car on her way out of the room and together she and John drove off in the car. This constituted a taking and carrying away. Their later action of selling the car to a third party is clear evidence of an intent never to return it to Jerry.

Thus a larceny was committed.

Modern Law Burglary of Car

Defined above.

Under modern law definitions, Jerry's car is a structure. When they entered it trespassorily (without permission), they committed a burglary, because their purpose in entry was to steal the car (a crime).

State v. Bob

After stealing the car, John and Jill took it to Bob's All-Night Car Sales, and sold it to Bob for $2,500.

Receiving Stolen Property

This crime occurs when there is a receipt of stolen property, knowing it is stolen, with intent to deprive the owner thereof.

Knowledge of the stolen nature of the car can be inferred from the circumstances. Here, Bob should have known the car was stolen, because it was brought to him late at night, and people rarely sell brand new cars for the low price of $2,500. Furthermore, Bob had already entered a deal to sell stolen cars to Jimmy, so he had requisite knowledge. He also actually received the car, and had the intent to deprive the owners by selling the car to a third party.

Thus, he is guilty of receiving stolen property.

Conspiracy to Sell Stolen Cars

Conspiracy defined above.

Jimmy had told Bob he would buy as many stolen cars as he could get his hands on. Bob sold the stolen car to him.

State will argue that a conspiracy existed: (1) There was an intent to agree and actual agreement that Bob would sell stolen cars to Jimmy, and (2) his act of selling the car in question was an overt act in furtherance of the conspiracy.

Bob will counter that Jimmy was an undercover agent and had no actual intent to agree; he will then claim that since two are required for a conspiracy, and since Jimmy did not agree, there was no conspiracy and he cannot be convicted.

Although Bob cannot be convicted under Common Law rules, the Model Penal Code provides for a unilateral conspiracy whereby a conspiracy exists as long as there is an agreement by the defendant.

Entrapment

A defendant is allowed to claim the defense of entrapment if he was induced by a police officer or other law enforcement agent to commit the crime. This defense is available for non-serious crimes where law enforcement officers entrapped the defendant. Under the traditional view, there is no defense as long as the defendant was already predisposed to commit the crime—the officer must create the intent to commit the crime. Under the modern objective view, courts look at the conduct of the law enforcement officer and find entrapment when the crime was committed in response to law enforcement activity that would be likely to cause a reasonable person to commit a crime.

While Bob may claim that Jimmy entrapped him by pretending to be interested in buying stolen cars, the state will show that (1) Bob was already predisposed to sell stolen cars, and (2) Jimmy did not engage in conduct that would entice a reasonable person to commit a crime.

Entrapment will not be a successful defense.

State v. Rachel

Receiving Stolen Property

Defined above.

State will try to argue that Rachel received stolen property when she bought the car from Jimmy, the undercover officer. They will argue that at the price of $4,000, she should have known the car was stolen, and by purchasing it she intended to deprive the owner.

However, Rachel will counter that she was never told the car was stolen, and furthermore that at the time she bought the car it was not stolen property since it had been recovered by law enforcement (Jimmy was an undercover agent). Even if the state finds the necessary elements of the crime of receiving stolen property, Rachel may assert the defense of entrapment.

Entrapment

Defined above.

Rachel was not already predisposed to buy the car, and it took Jimmy over five hours to convince her to buy it. Even then, she was reluctant. Therefore, this defense will be successful, and Rachel will not be guilty of receiving stolen property.

Attempt to Receive Stolen Property

An attempt is the substantial step toward perpetration of an intended crime.

Even though the legal classification of the car (recovered by the police) made commission of the crime of receiving stolen property factually impossible, courts have universally held that this is no defense against the crime of attempt to receive stolen property. However, Rachel will not be found guilty, because she can assert the entrapment defense discussed above.

State v. John

Aggravated Robbery

Robbery is the trespassory taking of another's personal property from his person or presence by violence or intimidation. Modern law distinguishes aggravated robberies, and one aggravating factor is when the robbery is committed with a deadly weapon.

Here, John stole Jerry's watch and billfold (personal property), from his person (took it from him personally), by force (at gunpoint). Furthermore, his use of a gun (deadly weapon) aggravated the crime.

John is guilty of aggravated robbery.

State v. Jill

Forgery

Forgery is the fraudulent making or altering of a writing of apparent legal significance with intent to defraud another.

Here, Jill forged Jerry's name on four checks with intent to defraud him by cashing them.

Voluntary Intoxication

While voluntary intoxication is not a specific defense to forgery, it can be used to negate specific intent. Thus, if Jill can show that as a result of her drinking heavily all afternoon she was unable to form the necessary intent, she may escape conviction for forgery.

Depending on whether Jill is successful in using her intoxication to negate the specific intent requirement, she may not be guilty of forgery.

Uttering

Uttering is offering as genuine an instrument known to be false, with intent to defraud.

Jill cashed the four checks (offered them as genuine) at four grocery stores around town with the intent to defraud Jerry of his money. Uttering is a specific intent crime. Therefore, Jill may also try to use voluntary intoxication to show she did not have the requisite intent here as well. Depending on whether this argument is successful, she may be guilty of uttering.

Modern Law Rule: While at Common Law, forgery and uttering were separate crimes, but modernly they are recognized as one crime.

Accomplice Liability

Accomplice liability will be found where one incites or facilitates the commission of a crime.

The state may argue that Jill and John should both be guilty of the robbery, forgery, and uttering, even though both parties did not actively participate in each of them. They may not have agreed with the crimes being committed; they should both be guilty based on an accomplice liability theory because they were present at the scene of the crimes. However, in order for a person to be guilty based on an accomplice liability theory, that person must have intended to commit the actual crime. It must be shown that the defendant gave some active encouragement; mere presence is not enough.

Jill did not encourage John to commit the robbery in any way; rather, Jill was shocked at John's actions. In addition, there are no facts indicating that John encouraged Jill to forge and cash the checks. Therefore, because it will be difficult for the state to show that Jill and John actively encouraged each other in the commission of the crimes, the state will not likely be successful on this claim.

What Makes the Second Answer Better?

As with torts, criminal law essay questions include many different, but mostly unrelated issues. While some crimes are related to others, as in the case of conspiracy or aggravated crimes, the elements of the crimes are distinct.

The main differences between the two sample answers are the number of crimes discussed and the quality of the analysis. The first answer was a good response, but it failed to include a discussion on conspiracy and the resulting liability under Pinkerton's Rule. It also did not address the possibility of accomplice liability.

In responding to any essay question, it very important to answer the call of the question and to follow instructions. In the first answer you will notice that the robbery of John was discussed before the crimes that Bob committed were discussed. This was contrary to the specific instructions given. Because the call of the question asked for a discussion of the potential outcomes for all the defendants, it was also important to analyze the defenses that a defendant could raise and how a court would likely rule regarding the defendant's guilt.